Franklyn S Haley

MY TIMES WITH THE SISTERS
AND OTHER EVENTS

by
Franklyn E. Dailey Jr.

Dailey International Publishers
19 Brookside Circle
Wilbraham, Massachusetts 01095
www.daileyint.com

The Year 2000

Author's Edition

**Copyright 2000
By Franklyn E. Dailey Jr.**

ISBN 0-9666251-1-0

First Printing May 2000
by Van Volumes, Ltd.
65 Springfield Street
Three Rivers, Massachusetts 01080

Cover by Claire Keefe

The author invites you to share the experiences of a boy growing up during the U.S. Constitutional experiment known as Prohibition. This book is dedicated to three Sisters of St. Joseph of Carondolet. From them, this boy learned to love his neighbor and his country, to work hard in school, and to fight only when there was no other choice.

I wish to remember my own Sis, with me for all but my first year of life. She left us on December 11, 1999.
> She always told folks that "my brother was an only child". Most never questioned her about it. Others knew the meaning it had for her, a wry, but loving brother statement.

To all Sisters and sisters everywhere: My appreciation for what you mean to man, and to mankind, increases every day.

March 19, 2000
Franklyn E. Dailey Jr
413-596-3752; www.daileyint.com; dailey@crocker.com

This is the author's second book. First published in 1998 by Dailey International Publishers and since reprinted three times, is "Joining The War At Sea 1939-1945" The ISBN is 0-9666251-0-2. This true story covers the Battle of the Atlantic and assault landings at Casablanca, Sicily, Salerno, Anzio and Southern France.

Acknowledgements

Print:
Booklet, Nativity of B.V.M School 1876-1976; cover by Eloise Wilkin

Daily Missal of the Mystical Body, Maryknoll Fathers 1957

The story "The Rochester, Lockport and Buffalo Railroad Corp. April 1919-April 1931" by William Reed Gordon, 811 Garson Ave. Rochester, N.Y., copyright 1963

Commemorative Booklet, Town of Sweden (New York) Sesqui-Centennial Celebration 1814-1964

Booklet, "Memories Of My Altar Boy Days 1962", published and copyrighted by Franklin X. McCormick, Milwaukee, WI, 1961

Paperback, "A Resident's Recollections" (of Rochester and Irondequoit, N.Y.) authored and copyrighted by Lloyd E. Klos, 1987. ISBN 0-932334-58-X

Photos:
(1) Church of the Nativity of the BVM and (2) School of the Nativity of the BVM; both obtained from Church Archives by Mary Gira; Martin R. Wahl Photographic Inc.,28 Woodbury Way, Fairport, N.Y. 14450

Personal:
Mary Gira, Public Relations Chairperson, Nativity BVM School; Margie Searl, Rochester Memorial Art Gallery

Table of Contents

List of Illustrations

My Times With The Sisters
And Other Events

Chapter One - An Incorporated Village

These events took place in a small town in western New York State not long after the end of World War I. "Small" is a relative term, so let me be as specific as the elders were to me when I would ask them the "size" question. The population of Brockport, New York was 3501 persons in 1929. "Town" is a generally used designation for settlements smaller than cities, but for this story, an "incorporated village" in the State of New York had important distinctions that I did not appreciate until later in life.

We lived at 48 South Avenue when I first became aware of an address. Our home later became 52 South Avenue for reasons that were never made clear to me. Our telephone number was 75. At night when our parents were out, we could ask the Telephone Operator when our parents would be home. "We" consisted of Sis and me. I was Frankie. Shortly, the phone would ring and the Operator would tell us when our mother and father would be coming home. Mother was Isabel Lasher Dailey and Dad was Franklyn E. Dailey. Dad's early school certificates, which I discovered in the suitcase that he left me, recorded his name as Franklin E. Dailey.

South Avenue came into Main Street opposite Brockway Place. As a family, we occasionally drove to Niagara Falls, Ontario to have dinner at the General

1

Brock Hotel there while enjoying its view of the falls. As a young boy, I pondered whether Brockport and Brockway might be connected with the Canadian General Brock of the War of 1812. The fact that the Canadians honored a man who might be connected with my town was one of those little puzzles that gathered in my mind over the years. I could have put the question to a search engine on the World Wide Web but why solve a lifelong riddle that I have enjoyed so much. (Later, I came across a booklet, "The Town of Sweden Sesqui-Centennial 1814-1964," which revealed that the town and the street are named for Hiel Brockway, the village founder, who migrated from Connecticut. So much for General Brock.)

Illustration 1 - The Village in the Twenties

BROCKPORT, N.Y.

In the period from 1925 to 1935, the Village of Brockport had two funeral homes and two furniture stores. There were three different ice cream brands available in town. The coupling of furniture and funeral provided the livelihood for two prominent Brockport families. Many years later, it gradually dawned on me that the relationship of funeral and furniture was not entirely a coincidence. In the experience of many small towns, people didn't die every day so the undertakers needed a steady business and furniture was often the choice. It seems reasonable that a competence in casket buying was extendible to furniture. A connoisseur of fine mahogany, oak or cherry in caskets could make that expertise work twice when selecting living room pieces. Which reminds me that all the caskets I saw as a very young man were in family living rooms or parlors, not in funeral home parlors. Mr. George Dunn ran one of these hybrid businesses and Mr. A.V. Fowler, our neighbor on South Avenue, ran the other.

Mr. Fowler owned a sour cherry orchard just east of the upper end of our street. That orchard was a stone's throw from the A&P Canning Factory at the end of Fair Street in Brockport. In my earliest employment summers, before I began a regular summer work/visit sojourn at my Grandfather Lasher's North Star Fruit Farm in North Wolcott, N.Y., I obtained cherry picking employment in A.V. Fowler's orchard. Hidden from the road but quite visible at the back of the orchard were his retired horse drawn hearses and an old ambulance carriage. What looked like dark dried blood on the floor of the ambulance carriage activated the imaginations of the younger cherry pickers.

For ice cream availability, FroJoy was the trade name used locally by Sealtest Ice Cream. Matheos Brothers had a creamery in Spencerport, the next burg in line toward Rochester (if you overlooked Adams Basin, a wide spot on the Erie Canal). Matheos operated a Greek ice cream shop under the Strand movie house at the corner of State and Main in Brockport. After a movie, especially if I had been able to "sneak in" and avoid parting with my dime too early, I would treat myself to a banana split courtesy of the Matheos Brothers and the defeated usher at the Strand. Bartholomay was a Rochester creamery. Their chocolate ice cream was my favorite. The Volstead Act, which enforced the ban on intoxicating liquors, was nullified with the repeal of the 18th amendment by the 21st Amendment. This allowed the Bartholomay plant to revert in 1933 to the beer brewing which it had been forced to give up in 1919. For 14 years, while the elders in my family and indeed in all of Brockport had to import the stuff illegally (rum running) from Canada across Lake Ontario, the younger among us benefited by having an extra source of good ice cream. Even when they got it back, the elders had to be content with 3.2% beer for the first year or two after repeal.

Brockport had four doctors, two dentists and two drug stores. Pharmacist Dobson had a soda counter in his drug store but Pharmacist Ed Simmons (not related to my neighbor Howard Simmons) did not have one. This was an important distinction to small fry. The main downtown blocks of businesses had two smoke shops, Decker's hardware store (Alfred Decker, the son, was valedictorian of my high school class), and a downtown bakery. Mr. Davis ran a small grocery market that stands out in my mind as the first place our townspeople, and especially my mother who was always an early adopter, could buy frozen vegetables. Birdseye was the brand. It was decades later that I discovered that there was a Mr. Birdseye.

I emphasize "downtown", as the site of Covert's Bakery. That enterprise certainly provided an appealing aroma for a small boy whose spirits were actually nourished by just walking by, which he did as often as possible. Covert's was on the west side of downtown's Main Street. Its bakery fumes were a perfect offset to the smoke shops on the east side of Main Street. For bake goods available to a near-addict, my own trade went to Mrs. Raleigh's, not just uptown but only two doors from our home on South Avenue. Her very dark molasses cookies with just a light sprinkle of sugar on top came from a wood stove that Charlie Raleigh, Kitty Raleigh's husband, had to re-supply frequently from a "wood pile out back."

The early inhabitants of Brockport were farmers and businessmen. It was no accident that the village was situated on the Erie Canal. When dug during the administration of Governor Dewitt Clinton, it was named the Erie Canal, sometimes derided by his detractors as Clinton's Ditch. After being known, during my stay at least, as the Barge Canal, its name reverted after I left town to its original "Erie" name. I swam there.

Brockport was on the Niagara Falls branch of the New York Central Railroad. I hiked along their tracks east of the populated section of town, frequently as my way to the Mt. Olivet Catholic Cemetery and the Soldier's Monument where I liked to browse. These venerable places adjoined each other a couple of miles east of town. The monument was dedicated in 1893 as the centerpiece of a Civil War Cemetery. It was already deteriorating in the late twenties. My companions and I considered it a little daring to go to the top of the Soldier's Monument whose spiral iron stairway was rusting and barely supported by stones set in now crumbling mortar. Fifty-two feet high, and only about 35 years old when I frequented it, the circular sandstone tower was already an abandoned relic.

I will likely repeat, too often for the reader I fear, that I was a hiker. Cemeteries were a favored destination. Mt. Olivet contained a grave of lasting memory. A seven-year-old Italian girl had died and the loving parents had added a statue of her in front of the granite family marker. Sculpted, and encased in clear glass, a small boy's view was the likeness of a girl of his age dressed in clothes of his age, who had already been taken from this world. South of Brockport, on the second lake escarpment south from town, was a larger cemetery built on the slope. There, I would often see my first Jack-in-the-Pulpit in the spring as the snows melted away. I would also experience the rancid odor of molded cut flowers placed on new graves the previous fall. In a later chapter, we will come to Brockport's main cemetery in town on High Street.

The next photo was taken from an 1895 New York Central Railroad brochure promoting sightseeing.

Illustration 2 -A Civil War Soldier's Monument

There was no fence and no flag by the time my generation visited the monument. Other hikers I encountered along those rail tracks carried burlap bags. Their mission was to retrieve coal dropped from a steam engine's coal car or from coal being transported in coal cars. Coal was dear and by 1930, times were tough.

Brockport was an Incorporated Village. I lived in many other places in the years following Brockport, but "Incorporated" in New York State in the 1920s equated to paved streets with curbs, sidewalks, streetlights, a tree belt and a sewer system. Thirty-five years later, in 1962, now with wife and growing family in an urban flight suburb of a Massachusetts city, I would become the owner of a brand new home. Surprise! This home had a septic tank and leach field. My early life had gone directly from outhouse to Brockport's village sewage system, with its primary and secondary treatment plant. I knew this sewage system firsthand because Brockport's filtration beds were on one of my regular eastbound hiking routes. My nose is as well tuned as anyone's. I accepted all the smells of Brockport, fresh tomatoes loaded onto horse drawn wagons, pea vine processing plants, newly cut alfalfa fields, bakeries and sewage as perfectly normal conditions of my environment. That was long before I encountered the word, "environment."

Our Incorporated Village was also the home of the Brockport Normal School. Subsequently it became Brockport State Teacher's College and then SUNY (for State University of New York) Brockport. This institution will be visited again in this story. Margie

Searl, an e-mail correspondent living in Rochester, New York, has informed me that there is a Dailey Hall there. Perhaps, like my wishful connection of Brockport to General Brock, this too might have turned out to have no connection with my family. In an examination of papers sent to me by Wendy Bennett of the Vincent Dailey family, (Aunt Corinne, my godmother, was married to my Uncle Vincent) I found a picture of Dailey Hall at SUNY. So, there must be something to Margie Searl's conjecture.

52, nee 48, South Avenue was on the very edge of town. Behind our house, open fields, broken by an occasional small grove of trees, flourished. This panorama was further defined by hardly discernible, rusted wire fencing held up by rotted, tottering posts. One other prominent break consisted of three willow trees in a line along one of the north-south section lines. Beneath those trees was a fresh water spring that often re-invigorated a hot, tired, and usually dirty little boy. In the winter months, those springs made for skating. Expect to fall through and get a "footwet" if you ventured too close to the spring. Mr. Lawler, a South Avenue neighbor, owned the lot to the east of the three willow trees. His lot could be accessed through a hole in his wire fence. Just inside the lot, there was a well. Mr. Lawler kept milk cows and the well was used to keep a broad circular wooden water trough full for his cows. Also prominent there were two or three blocks of salt laying on the ground for the cows.

Dunkie Smith, Mr. Lawler's grandson, used to take his visiting Michigan cousins down to that cow pasture for corn silk smoking, and later for smoking real cigarettes. The Michigan cousins were well known on South Avenue because during their visits they were allowed to drive the family car. In Michigan at the time, no driver's licenses were necessary. We New York kids were jealous because we were some years from driving due to New York's license requirements and their stringent enforcement. Dunkie had the last laugh though. The Michigan kids got sick from smoking and Dunkie, who was immune from such distress probably due to his greater experience in the vice, not only did not seem sympathetic, he seemed to have a little smirk on his face.

Any boy who has completely soaked his shoes by falling through the ice will understand what it was like to wear them on succeeding days, until the effect "wore off." Likely, the shoes never recovered; the boy just got used to the new feeling on his feet.

I had a hand-me-down pair of hockey skates and a "boughten" pair of racing tube skates. When I was quite young, Uncle Norman came to visit. He brought me a gift. A hockey stick. Uncle Norman Lasher stayed quite awhile, and left only after he relapsed into one of his catatonic periods. Those became evident to me at the dinner table where he would neither eat nor respond to any conversation. I did not know the word then, but Uncle Norman had schizophrenia. A World War I vet of the Coast Guard, Uncle Norman had become unwelcome at Grandfather Lasher's home, especially after Grandfather took his second wife, Aunt Elsa. Seems that Harry Lasher was willing to provide support for his son Norman, but no longer in his own home. After many episodes of being farmed out, the earliest of which was to a prominent military prep school in Indiana, Uncle Norman finally settled in at the Canandaigua (New York) Veterans Hospital. Forty years later there he died. My mom, attired in her Red Cross Gray Lady uniform, visited her brother for all of those years. Occasionally, Mother took me along. I have Uncle Norman's watch, his small AM/FM early transistor radio and the American Flag supplied to vets at their death. I am really sorry that I no longer have that hockey stick. It was a prized possession, probably surrendered when leaving one of too many abodes along the way of life. We also have Mom's Gray Lady uniform. I keep asking myself how she could have been that small.

All this is merely backdrop for the culture and caring of the Sisters of St. Joseph. I came from a dysfunctional family long before that term was in use. No, don't blame Uncle Norman. He had no responsibility for the alcohol and stock market excesses that marred my father's contribution to the life of *young-marrieds*. The courtship and wedded period for my father and mother began with the Volstead Act and included the stock market crash of 1929 and the bank failures of 1933. The Sisters were my salvation. I convey that in the vernacular sense and therefore did not capitalize the word, "salvation." I am not trying to prejudge what the Lord has in store for me. Then again, the Sisters always urged us to "pray for a happy death." I still do.

"My times" involved being late for school more than a few of those times. In those days you could, if you lived anyplace inside the town, be late twice a day. Walk to school. Many points of interest. Walk home for lunch. Variations in many points of interest. Walk back to school. More points of interest. You get the picture. I was late quite often. After leaving the Sisters and their school in 1932, I went to Brockport High School, then located in a few spare classrooms on an upper floor of the Brockport Normal School. Brockport's new high school, built in 1934-35, is where I went for the last half of my last year in high school, graduating in 1935. That high school was later converted to a middle school bearing the name A.D. Oliver, Brockport High's Principal while I was there. Jack Milner, the Principal of the A.D. Oliver Middle School during its reconstruction and re-dedication, opened the original 1935 cornerstone box before the 1997 celebration event commemorating the building's remodeling. In the box, resting for 62 years, he found a "late pass" for Frank Dailey.

Brockport had three schools that delivered eight grades of primary school education. An integral part of the Brockport Normal School was a school known as the Training School. Here, the young teachers in training in the Normal School obtained their OJT, a teacher's "on the job training," in a fully accredited primary school. These fledgling teachers did this under the eye of ladies known as "Critics." Some of these Critics boarded with Mrs. Birdsall just across the street from our home on South Avenue. These ladies arrived in September, left in June. I met many of them and they seemed to be very nice ladies. I must admit I had a hard time with the dictionary word, "critic," because its meaning did not seem to fit those very nice ladies across the street. Then again, I never set foot in the Training School schoolrooms where the Critics performed their duties. The student teachers may have viewed the Critics quite differently.

As noted, I met these Critic ladies a number of times. They were neighbors and they boarded with Mrs. Birdsall, the widowed mother of Mrs. Herbert Lane who lived with her husband and family in the third house up the street from her mother. It is not necessary for the reader to keep track of all the relationships in this small town. I had some difficulty following them when I lived there.

What I can easily recall was the primary reason I found to visit each of these homes, where, I am happy to say I was always welcome. Mrs. Birdsall's specialty was sour cream cookies with raisins. I never tired of them and the only charge was to be nice to the boarders when I came. And since I liked people, being nice came easy. Mrs. Birdsall also 'put up' canned fruits using a product called Certo. If you can still find Certo being used in a home, you'll know that something good is going on.

Brockport's Parochial School completed the trio of primary education facilities in our village. The next illustration is a sketch of the school taken from the cover of a booklet prepared for the celebration of the 100th anniversary of the school's founding in 1876.

Illustration 3- School of the Nativity of the BVM

1915

Diagonally across from the School of the Nativity of the Blessed Virgin Mary that I attended, stood the

Brockport Grammar School. That gray stone building occupied a lot at the southwest corner of Utica and Holley Street. I passed the front of that building several thousand times while making my way north or south on Utica Street to and from the Catholic School. Occasionally, a shout from the Grammar School playground across Utica Street would reach my ears that identified me as a "cat licker." I also became aware that the Sisters were sometimes referred to as "black crows."

While I set forth here experiences with the Sisters of St. Joseph, my thoughts extend to all Sisters who have nourished the spirits, the minds and the bodies of millions of young children in this great country. My wife and I are the grateful recipients of ministrations in schools and hospitals from caring Sisters of Charity, Sisters of Mercy and Sisters of the Holy Cross. Our eight children have known the nurturing of devoted Sisters of many orders throughout the United States. My sister, Alma, received her education from the Madames of the Sacred Heart.

A 19th century photo of Brockport's first Parochial School can be found in the booklet prepared for the Town of Sweden Sesqui-Centennial Celebration in 1964. To a graceful, existing, home dwelling which the first Sisters used as their convent, there was added a T-shaped structure at the rear. This was erected in 1875. This was the school my father attended. It was located on the southwest corner of Utica and Erie Street and faced on Utica Street. The buildings were in an advanced state of deterioration when I was in them in the 1920s and have since been torn down.

One of the rich memories I have of my father was being with him on several occasions when he visited the home of Charlotte Elizabeth Martin. I recall that there was no setback to her Erie Street home from the street. Once inside, her home was cool and quite appealing, the house having been favored by some lovely old shade trees, a feature of the village. That house was in the block between Main Street and Utica Street on the south side of Erie Street, just a few doors from the original Catholic Church. I was strictly along for company on the trip, perhaps because there was no one else home at the time, or because my Dad sensed that something important was occurring there and it would be good for me to be present. Charlotte Martin was interviewing Dad on the origins of the Dailey family and their presence in the Town of Sweden, the township that included the village of Brockport. I learned later that Charlotte Martin had tried in vain to get the village to celebrate its 100th birthday in 1929. Failing that she determined to write the history herself and left us "The Story of Brockport for One-Hundred Years 1829-1929." Her paragraph on the Parochial School reads as follows:

"In September, 1873, a large house and spacious grounds were purchased of Mrs. M.M. Sadler, widow of one of the most prominent men of early times, and sister of E.B. Holmes. This site was for the home of a convent and parochial school. On January 10, 1876, the school was opened in a large school house erected on the same lot during the year 1874-75 under the supervision of Sisters Ursula, Louise and Agatha. The present Parochial School was built in 1915."

In the twenties, the new brick school having been dedicated in 1915, the now-abandoned first Parochial school building was used for bazaars (known today as "fundraisers.") Games and raffles on the day of the event had been preceded by weeks of door to door solicitation of pennies for raffle chances. These chances originated on cardboard backs salvaged from writing pads. Onto this cardboard, numbered squares would be pencilled in. For pennies proffered to the pupil doing the soliciting, the giver's name was scrawled into a like number of squares. Then the squares (chances) were cut up and put in the hopper to be fished out for prize-winners. I sold plenty of chances to the raffles. If I ran out of tickets, I would just go get my own tablet, tear off the cardboard back, and with my ruler scribe out some more chances. Townspeople of all faiths gave enthusiastic support to these drives. Some even asked me ahead of time when I'd be coming around to their front door. Fudge sales were a favorite cash generator at the bazaar. Fudge was not raffled but sold outright. My mother was a good cook but did not bake. She did make fudge on request and I would take it to the old school hall and give it to Sister. In the first hour after the bazaar opened, my Mom would be down to buy her own fudge back. She did not quite trust the kitchen skills of Catholic mothers.

The Sisters conducted some sort of money-raising activity throughout the school year. My favorite was the chocolate covered peppermint patties for one cent. Not just a good value as they were, but if your patty had a pink center instead of white, you received five patties free. It put you to looking for pennies to buy patties. People who look for money usually find some. To this day, I see money on the street as I ride my bike. In those days, one sure way to find money was to go downtown, take the gum out of your mouth, attach it to a piece of string, and drop it down through the sidewalk grates and "fish" for coins. Not just pennies but sometimes nickels, dimes and even a quarter. Half dollars were often too heavy to hold onto the gum during the process but they were worth going home and getting some heavy equipment for the job.

The mid-twenties had been an era of prosperity for almost everyone in Brockport. Buying new cars was a favorite pastime. The well-to-do men were attracted to cylinders. Cadillacs and Packards were popular and some had twelve or even sixteen cylinders. Most cars were black, and polishing was a highly visible and almost sacred ritual. Chauffeurs would make their car as prominent as possible in the master's driveway and small fry were invited for looks under the hood. There were even a few electrics around, usually driven by ladies very intent on their course. Later, as a student naval aviator, I recall the instruction to constantly employ "peripheral vision." That instruction is remembered in contrast to the lady electric car drivers who clenched the steering lever and had their eyes riveted forward. In our family's early car parade, I can recall both Model T and Model A Fords, an Auburn (the poor man's Cord) and a Chrysler 60. Coal was still being delivered by horse driven wagon and all local produce moving toward the A&P Canning Factory up our street was delivered in wagons. Ice and milk were delivered and garbage taken away in wagons. The first trucks that I recall were chain-driven Macks, with solid rubber tires on wheels with wooden spokes. Those tires had cylindrical holes bored crossways to give the driver some relief from bumps but drivers made it clear to us kids that while the intent was good, those wheels never took the bump out of a bump. Dailey Coal and Produce lost several horses in a stall fire in one of the earliest incidents of my recall. Dad told me that horses did not know which way to go in a fire. Photos of flaming horses appeared in news accounts. Not long after this fire, our coal was delivered in trucks. An early model coal truck discharged the coal sidewise to empty into a chute that was directed into a basement window. The engine driven truck did not arrive too soon to keep Sis and me from several years of joint February birthday parties whose feature would be a horse drawn sleigh-ride. The hay filled sleigh bed was a coal or produce carrier on weekdays before the machine age arrived. These celebrations occurred before the money slipped away.

Part of the learning experience for a boy in a Parochial School was his introduction to the Latin for serving Mass. Each of the remaining chapters of this story will begin with this first Latin that I learned. My learning experience came in the summer between the first and second grade, the summer of 1927 for me. Sister Emma taught me a soft pronunciation of Latin, more like an Italian would pronounce the words. The "c" sounds were soft, not like k's. In the Brockport High

School, beginning in 1932, I took Latin 1, Latin II (Caesar) and Latin III (Cicero). I had to do some relearning of the pronunciation. My wonderful Latin teacher there, Miss Esther Shulman, taught us Germanic sounds and Caesar came out more like Kae-sar than the Cee-zar-ee-an we meet in the Passion each Lent. I have placed the English translations after the Latin. Much later came the discovery for me that the English phrases were quite beautiful. These passages are still relevant in the Mass today, and would be powerful words if used in more of our human discourse.

Chapter Two - Prelude to School

Introibo ad altare Dei.
Ad Deum qui laetificat juventutem meam.

I will go into the altar of God,
To God who gives joy to my youth.

My first awareness of the Sisters occurred in late 1925 or early 1926, the year before I started first grade. The first time I can recall being in their presence took place in the original Church of the Nativity of the Blessed Virgin Mary (BVM) located at the southeast corner of Utica and Erie streets in Brockport, New York.

I was going-on five years old. The Sisters were already seated together for Sunday Mass when Dad brought me into the church for the first time. After attending a few Sunday Masses with my Dad, I knew where to look for the Sisters because they always occupied the same pews. Mother did not go to Mass with us. She had been brought up a Lutheran but joined St. Luke's, the Episcopal Church in Brockport. Mom liked Father Veazey and his wife, Carol. Mother also played piano and organ and they had a need for that over at St. Luke's. My sister, Alma 'Sis' Dailey, joined Dad and me at Sunday Mass about one year after I first began going to Mass with Dad.

21

Before I get too far into a story about the Sisters, I'd better tell you a little about my mother and father. I owe much to the six years God gave me with a small group of remarkable, loving, teaching Sisters of St. Joseph who took on the burden of second parents. I do not want the reader to conclude that I think any the less of my parents because of the recognition I give to the enormous part the Sisters played in my life.

Dad was the ninth and last child, and eighth son, of William Dailey and Jessie McGarry Dailey, if you leave out Henry who died at birth. William had been the sixth of nine in the family of John and Mary Dailey who migrated with their first three children from Ireland in 1836. Family, do not hold me responsible for the spelling of Jessie's maiden name. It appears as McGarry from Patrick McGarry, her grandfather, in a printed genealogy found in my Dad's Gladstone bag. It appears as McGearry on the gravestones in Holy Sepulchre Cemetery in Rochester, New York. McGearry is found on Jessie's gravestone and on her maiden sister's (Anna's) stone. Brockport historian Charlotte Elizabeth Martin, after her discussions with my father, recorded it as McGary. I do not know if it was a specialty of the Irish, but their name spellings in my family reveal some tinkering throughout the 1850-2000 period that I have examined. Family speculation centers on County Mayo in Ireland as our family origin and my father told me that O'Dalaigh was the Gaelic spelling of our name.

The Dailey family has a large plot in Holy Sepulchre Cemetery in Rochester New York. Eleven caskets were transferred there on July 20, 1917, a date marking the opening of the plot. A most telling message is found in the grave markers of my father's father and mother, two of his brothers and his sister. These reveal 1918-1921 as an extraordinary death period. Rochester's Riverside Cemetery is the next cemetery down the Genesee River, adjacent to Holy Sepulchre. In Riverside, lies my mother's mother who passed away in 1918. My mother is also there, having separated from my father in the early 1940s due to Dad's alcoholism.

Dad's brothers Jim and George died in the flu epidemic of 1918-19 and his sister Bertha died giving birth to her second child, all these events occurring before my birth. I really knew in the course of my younger life only five of Dad's brothers. In order of their age, they were John F. Dailey who was the first born child in that family, and William G. Dailey, Vincent Dailey, Donald A. Dailey and Jesse Oswald "Oz" Dailey, the 5th, 6th, 7th, and 8th children respectively. My Dad was $9^{th.}$ Local trips west from Brockport would bring a visit to Uncles John F. in Buffalo and William G. in Albion, New York. Trips east would take me to Rochester to see Uncle Don who lived on Canterbury Road and Uncle Vincent who lived on Grand Avenue in Rochester before moving to New York City. I was in Uncle Oz' home in Rochester a few times and much more frequently in his home in Brockport when he moved back there. I had just one sibling, my sister Alma "Sis" Dailey. Most of my in-family playtime occurred with Tom, Uncle Oz' second son and occasionally with his brother Oz who was older. I played a little with

Betty, Tom's sister, but she beat me so regularly at tennis that it became embarrassing.

As noted earlier, Dad was born Franklin but died Franklyn. I was baptized Francis but have known only the name Franklyn Jr. Mother was the third child of Harry Lasher and Alma Valentin Lasher. Alma Valentin came from Denmark. Harry Lasher's way back ancestor was Conrad Lasher, who was born in 1749 and died in 1824. He was a 2nd Lt., 1st Reg. Dutchess County, New York. I found this out from Mother's application, discovered in the suitcase she left me, to join the DAR. She had established that her eligibility was defined by descent from "a man or woman who, with unfailing loyalty to the cause of American Independence, served as a sailor, or as a soldier or civil officer in one of the several Colonies or States...." Apparently, Mom wearied of the application procedure. Having completed and put in writing her lineage investigation on a form supplied by the DAR, reaching back to Conrad in Germantown, NY in 1749, she failed to finish the last couple of lines of the required application.

Mom and Dad were married in late April of 1920 in the sacristy of the original Church of the Nativity of the BVM, in Brockport, New York. Mother confided to me more than once that she had to "sign a paper." In that paper, she had agreed to raise her children in the Catholic faith. Mother carried out her part of the bargain, making many sacrifices to do so. Though never a Roman Catholic, Mother later became a devout Anglican Catholic with a zealot's interest in "high" church and the "old" rite, to the dismay of some of her fellow Episcopalians. For the last 40 years of her 93-year life, Mother was all but a Roman Catholic. It has occurred to me that only the cold tones of her marriage ceremony in that sacristy in 1920 kept her from going all the way. There is no picture that I can find of that wedding. Judging from the wealth of photo albums left behind, both Mother and Dad took a lot of pictures with George Eastman's relatively new sensation, the box camera and the folding box camera. I have one camera of each model dating from 1921 along with albums and loose prints in great quantity. But, I cannot find a wedding picture. Forbidden, perhaps, for a mixed marriage in those days? Or the sacristy in the old church was simply too dark on that April Saturday night. I have the certificate signed by the Reverend Michael J. Krieg that he performed the nuptials for Franklyn E. Dailey and Isabel Lasher. Dad's older brother Oz signed as one witness and Mother's older sister, Martha, signed as the other witness.

Mother expressed to me many times her complete approval of the Sisters of St. Joseph. Praise did not come easily from Mother. Following her father's second marriage, my mother and her two sisters and brother were eased out of the second wife's new household. This experience led Mother to cast the female in the role of adversary in any situation where it was not crystal clear in whose body the villain resided. Again, the Sisters were always absolved even when remotely connected with one of Mother's prejudices.

As I grew and learned to know my mother, I realized that the Sisters, in our town, the Sisters of St. Joseph of

Carondolet, held special respect from my mother. While Mother was always reserved in praise or in criticism, I could tell that the Sisters were something special in her view of life. Mother favored discipline and the Sisters had discipline. For many years, Mother viewed the Sisters as something the Roman Catholic Church had that her Episcopalians did not have. Her priest, in those days Father Veazey of St. Luke's, was easily the equal of Father Krieg at the Roman Catholic Church. Mother regarded Episcopal Church parishioners as more than the equal of those attending the Church of The Nativity of the Blessed Virgin Mary. Mother was afflicted with her 'proper bringing up' form of bigotry. Most non-Catholic Christians have had a problem with the Real Presence, but only a few dwell on it and my Mother did not. We Roman Catholics had the Sisters and that made a difference in her mind. As Mom grew in life and in understanding, more and more she referred to her church as Anglican Catholic. Then, at a crucial time later in her life, she made a retreat. And on that retreat, Mother made the discovery that the Anglicans had Sisters. Mother Virginia and my mother corresponded until my Mother died. I really believe that at the time of her discovery of an order of Anglican Sisters, Mom's religious life became filled out, complete. She would need no more on the road to meet her Maker. She never retreated from her respect for the Sisters of St. Joseph, but she took much solace that her church also had a place for Sisters.

I mentioned bigotry. It was not blatant in my mother. But it did creep out once in awhile. When I visited her many years after World War II, then having a growing family of my own, I was witness to a dialogue between Mother and some of her friends from Brighton, a suburb of Rochester, and one of the first places of urban flight from that city. Brighton High School was singled out, just as many are today, for its exceptional students. Brighton was the place where Kodak managers on the rise settled, and as with those exposed to educated adults, the children simply absorbed knowledge faster. Another facet of urban living was that most of the students at Brighton High were bused to school. Just at the time of this visit with my mother, the Diocese of Rochester was involved in a school building program that included a new Parochial school connected with St. Thomas More Church, a relatively new Catholic parish in Brighton. Mother's friends expressed their fear that the Catholic kids who would be bused to the new school would be throwing papers and other trash out the window of the bus on its way to the new school. Mother appeared to agree. I interjected and pointed out to my Mother that the Brighton public school kids were just as likely as the Catholic kids to be throwing stuff out the bus windows and I opined that the likelihood was low in both cases. Mother got pretty upset with me for pointing that out in front of her friends. It turned out to be a conversation closer.

Although Mother had been warned by her father that there was "alcohol" in Dad's family, Mother married him anyway. Perhaps, almost because of her criticism of her father for marrying the Canadian lady we came to know as "Aunt Elsa", my mother may have become all the more determined to marry Dad. In later years, Aunt Elsa became my friend and my mother relented somewhat so as not to spoil my relationship with Elsa.

I was not present for my parent's courtship of course, but Grandfather Harry Lasher, Mother's Dad, was correct. There *was* alcohol in the Dailey family. Some of the Dailey family's flu related deaths in the death period of 1918-1919 were undoubtedly hastened by alcohol. Though my Dad lived until age 79 in 1975, the first part of his adult life encased the living hell of alcohol, leading to the failure of his marriage.

Alcoholics Anonymous extended Dad's life by at least 30 years. He had been in and out of the Monroe County Hospital and the New York State Hospital, both located in Rochester New York, many times, when "Bill" of AA came to Rochester in 1941 and helped Dad begin the first Rochester, New York chapter of the remarkable AA movement.

I had some intimate insights into Dad's hospital experiences. The wards housing the unruly stimulated a young boy's imagination. I made my own way around at a young age because there was most often no one to escort me. Entrance to these hospital wards generally took one to a heavy oak door that had a tiny wire-screened window at eye level. Through this window, an attendant would first look to see if you should be granted admission. Once inside, the patients, all in identical seersucker bathrobes, each provided me with furious mind-speculation as to what their problem was. Some men were pretty banged up and that made those visits even more fascinating. Dad related to me some details on the application of processes known as insulin shock therapy and electrotherapy that he had witnessed while incarcerated for alcohol abuse. He also told me some of the effects. Since Dad stayed in those hospitals with some frequency, I surmised later that Dad might have felt he was being evaluated as a potential candidate for one of those treatments. Anyone who has seen the play or movie of "One Flew Over The Cuckoo's Nest" pretty much has the picture that I have carried with me for seventy years.

Dad and Mom separated just as he was getting straightened out and Dad then went to live with a lady he met in AA. Mrs. "Kitty" Kelly had two small daughters. As a recovering alcoholic, Dad fulfilled with the Kelly family the duties of fatherhood that he frequently had skipped with our family.

We will see something of Dad in the first part of my 1926-1932 Parochial School period, much less in the second part because of alcohol. After about 1930, my parents were involved in my life and my sister's life, at best serially, and at worst not at all. My times with the Sisters covers my age from five to eleven, but the times when just one or even no parents were aboard at 52 South Avenue covers our ages from about eight to about 14. One day my Sis answered the front door bell at our 52 South Avenue, Brockport, New York home. In the vestibule was Mother returning after two years in New York City where she worked in Stern's Department store on 34th Street and lived at a YWCA house called Tatham House in Manhattan. Sis looked through the glass in the inner vestibule door, and would not let Mom in. Sis did not recognize who was at the door.

Near the end of his life, when Dad had been diagnosed with cancer that had spread to the spine, I went back to Rochester to help find a nursing home for his final months of life. One of Mrs. Kelly's daughters, who was then approaching thirty years old, accompanied me on a one-day tour of several prospective nursing homes in Rochester, New York. It was 1975, and a bad period for those establishments. The smell of urine pervaded the halls of every institution we visited. This young lady was moved to tears, saying repeatedly, "Daddy can't live in a place like this." More than once on that day, I was on the verge of saying, "Whose Daddy is this, anyway?" The Sisters must have dispatched the guardian angel that kept those words from crossing my lips. My pop was the only Daddy this girl knew.

Dad was the youngest of nine and his mother's favorite. He always spoke of her in saintly terms. He was a Catholic, he told me, simply because of his mother's deep faith. He told me of trips he took with his mother on the New York Central Railroad from Brockport through Rochester to Canandaigua, New York, where there was a connection to the Pennsylvania Railroad south to Harrisburg, Baltimore and Washington. His mother frequently needed to go to Johns Hopkins in Baltimore for radium treatments that kept her alive until she died from cancer late in 1921.

Grandfather William Dailey was the founder of the family coal and produce businesses. He persuaded

National Biscuit Company to build a shredded wheat cereal plant in Niagara Falls to which he could supply the hard wheat needed. He passed on in 1919 so my Dad became his mother's companion for her late-life cancer therapy trips.

I made weekend trips to the nursing home we selected for Dad in Rochester on Winton Road South from Decoration Day in 1975 until he died in early November that year. One weekend in September, Dad informed me that his nephew, Murray, eldest son of Dad's oldest brother John F. Dailey, but in age Dad's contemporary, made the suggestion that since Dad's cancer was inoperable, perhaps he would like a drink. Dad obviously took this very seriously and did not act on the suggestion before he passed it by me, putting it in the form of the question, "Should he or shouldn't he?". The contrasts of Dad's life with alcohol and later as a recovering, non-drinking alcoholic, flashed before my mind. This occurred on a Saturday morning so I asked Dad if I could reflect on it over night and let him know when I came back on Sunday morning. The sweats visited me all that night at a local motel. The next morning, I said to him, "Dad, that drink is not going to be as good as the prospect might appear to be. I recommend you put the thought aside." I am quite sure he did not break the string of thirty years of sobriety. We never discussed it again. He was gone in just a few weeks. It may seem farfetched but I believe that the reasoning infused with Grace that the sisters taught helped me handle a hard question. Inwardly, I was not too pleased with Murray for coming up with that idea.

It is a dignifying experience to have your Dad ask you a serious question. He had certainly answered some of mine. In late December 1945, Peggy, my wife, our first born, Franklyn III, an infant of two months, and I were proceeding north from Pensacola Florida where I had just received my Navy wings. It was three days before Christmas and we were traveling to Peggy's family home at Willoughby Spit near Norfolk Virginia. It was a day of ice-bound North Carolina roads in which our '35 Hudson Terraplane labored under the strain of everything we owned piled on its roof. It was also a day when the Greyhound bus drivers told me the ice was so bad they were not running. God was with us and we arrived at South Boston Virginia late in the afternoon. We put up at the town's only hotel, being given a dark mahogany room out of the Victorian age. I went to the lobby to the pay phone and put in a progress call to Peggy's home. Her mother answered, and, forbidding me to tell her, told me that Peggy's father had died that morning from a sudden heart attack. I tried to console Mrs. "May" Parker but I was dumbstruck from the gravest personal news of my life. Before going back to the room, I called my Dad and asked him what I should do. He came right back, "You've got to tell her." I did, and we cried together all night with an infant between us. Dad had the right advice. I knew this for certain when we rolled up the Parker driveway the next day and saw the casket in the living room window.

I discovered graphic evidence of Grandmother Dailey's favoritism. In the Gladstone bag that Dad gave me before he died, I found a handsome 5x7 framed picture of him. I kept it on my dresser. That frame always seemed slightly heavy though it appeared to have a light graceful construction. One day, when I held the frame up, two other pictures behind Dad's picture slipped out. These proved to be photos of two of Dad's older brothers neatly stored under Dad's photo. This thrifty Irish lady, Jessie McGarry Dailey, had found a way to get her youngest son's picture into a standing frame for display on her dresser without going out and buying yet another frame. And without throwing away the older brother's photos.

My mother learned from Jessie too. Mom told me that Jessie Dailey, her mother-in-law, had come to see me in Rochester a few months after my birth in February 1921. The scene was a Harvard flat (two up and two down) on Farrington Place next to the original Rochester Tennis Club. Mother had prepared a nice dinner to impress Dad's mother. There was unease at the table because I was crying in my crib. Mother and Dad told Jessie to please ignore this distraction, that the "new" method was to "let them cry it out." According to my mother's retelling of this event, Grandmother immediately went to the bedroom and rocked me to sleep. The small group then had a comfortable dinner. In passing on this story to me, my mother was honestly, if reluctantly, disclosing that the episode had made an impression on her. I suspect the new method was junked that evening.

I had come along in early February 1921. You can work out the math. In 1999, I attended my World War II destroyer's reunion at Atlantic City. Walking the boardwalk, I discovered the Claridge Hotel, the place Dad and Mom told me was the hotel where they had their honeymoon in April of 1920. My sister was born in February 1922, almost exactly one year after me. That was it for our family.

My times with the Sisters will cover the years 1926-1932. The recollections of the first part are pretty upbeat, but the mire of drinking, the consequent poverty, and depression in and outside of the family, may color the last part. The Sisters helped keep my little ship on course despite some severe buffeting.

The Sisters provided order and structure and love. My mother was an order and structure person and that was the attraction the sisters had for her. At home, Mom mostly got chaos. Don't get me wrong. For an order and structure person, Mother liked a little fling herself once in awhile. There was an element to the "wet" tide of those days that appealed to my Mother; I could sum it up with the expression, "If you can't beat 'em, join 'em."

Those Brockport parties were something to behold, as Sis and I did through the registers (adjustable grates) that brought heat from the first to the second floor of our home. Mother's wedding present was a Chickering baby grand piano. There were candles on the piano. I could tell when they had been used because I found the melted wax beneath them the next morning.

For the first couple of party hours, Mother played jazz age music. I have a three-foot stack of worn sheet music from those times. Dr. Hazen played the ukulele and insurance agency owner Bud Bruce played the saxophone. The sliding double doors to the patio would be opened up for dancing.

Between dances, Mother played songs like "Kitten on the Keys," Wedding of the Painted Doll," and "Nola." Her audience loved it. Some years later, Mother brought the sheet music for Peter deRose's "Deep Purple." While she kept limber with piano exercises by Grieg, Chopin, and others, she confessed to me that Deep Purple was not easy to play. I recall that she worked hard at it and finally felt satisfied that she was doing it justice.

Eventually, at those parties, the booze took hold and interesting things happened. Some of the booze was medicinal, that is, legitimate stuff that was almost legal. Remember that a Doctor was in the crowd. Next day, looking over the bare basement room where the booze was kept, I could find empty bottles that had been legitimately tax stamped at one time but had been recycled with "whatever" a number of times.

It was in that room during my fourth grade year that I tried to make root beer with Hires Root Beer Mix and Fleischmann's Yeast. I did not have a vat big enough for the whole formula so I had to proportion the mix. I did not get it quite right and I had no capping tool so used corks. For weeks afterward, a sound like a gun going off was a regular occurrence as the "strong" side of the batch blew their corks into the basement ceiling. At least I was able to give those retired bottles one last whirl. They may have survived only because I had to use corks.

One nerve wracking aftermath of those parties would be the challenge for some of its attendees to 'get going' the next morning by indulging in a bit of a follow-on. Mother watched Dad like a hawk during the early hours of the parties but at some hour of the evening her own enjoyment made her less vigilant. The next day began the vigil that was repeated countless times in my young life. One recollection is Dad coming home from the office for lunch. If he was chewing gum, and he frequently was, it would be a dead give-away. Sober, Dad was never a gum chewer.

Chapter Three - A Church Is Built

Adjutorium nostrum in nomine Domini.
Qui fecit caelum et terram.

Our help is in the name of the Lord.
Who has made heaven and earth.

After the Celebrant recited his Confiteor Deo Omnipotenti (I *confess to God...that I have sinned...*), the Altar Boys responded:
Misereatur tui omnipotens Deus, et, dimissis peccatis tuis, perducat te ad vitam aeternam.
May almighty God have mercy on you, forgive you your sins, and bring you to life everlasting.

(There is an author discovery process going on here. I noted earlier that I would introduce all but the first chapter of this story with the Altar Boy's responses to the Priest-Celebrant's intonations at Mass. The passage above includes the celebrant's Confiteor, the "I Confess" passage, right after the beginning of Mass, as the Celebrant prepares for what is to come. The Altar Boy is responding, "Misereatur tui....," not just for himself but for all those present at Mass including himself. I learned as I went back into an old Missal to make sure that my memory did not play tricks on me, that the pronouns in the Latin, after the Misereatur, are tui, tuis, and te, all Latin forms of a word translatable to the English word "you." What the Altar Boy is doing, on behalf of those

37

assembled, is forgiving "you", the Priest. In all my days of serving at Mass, that fact had escaped me. I cannot now recreate the relationship I had with the Pastor in the context that I was forgiving him. Readers may appreciate this as they get a little further into the story.)

My interest in the Sisters during the short period, at the most two years, of attending the old church was born of curiosity. Their garb, known as habits, and their togetherness marked them for my examination during Mass.

The first Catholic Church in Brockport faced on Erie Street. Down the center of Erie Street (brick pavement) were tracks which carried the trolley that operated between Rochester, New York some 18 miles to the east, and Lockport, New York, some 40 miles to the west. The trolley entered Brockport on State Street from the east, originating in Rochester and stopping in Spencerport before arriving in Brockport. The streets of our little village ended on Main Street and even if a street was exactly opposite, it always took on a different name in the crossover. So, the trolley exited Brockport to the west on Erie Street though it had arrived from the east on State Street. Same street as far as those tracks were concerned. Automobile drivers who become frustrated looking for a street that they are actually already on should avoid Brockport.

That trolley interested me and occasionally one went by when Sunday Mass was letting out. As I see my youngest grandchildren in comparable settings today, I have a flashback to that first Catholic Church. I was certain that the trolleys went by for my benefit. William

Reed Gordon wrote the story of this line in 1963. It existed as The Buffalo, Lockport and Rochester Railway from 1908-1919 and as the Rochester, Lockport and Buffalo Railroad Corp. from 1919-1931. Mr. Gordon recounted a large number of wrecks and even more 'incidents' during those years. Although the General Railway Signal Company was a Rochester business success selling equipment to the "steam" lines as they were dubbed by their electrified rail competitors, the latter shunned automated signal equipment; its motormen ran on "train instructions."

Illustration 4-Rochester, Lockport & Buffalo R.R. Corp.

Rear end of 501 at one of Brockport stations

In Illustration Four, the rear of the trolley line's Car 501 is pictured headed east for Rochester on State Street in Brockport, New York. The light toned brick building on the left houses the Strand Theatre along its entire second story. The theatre entrance was on Main Street in the foreground out of the camera's view. Visible in the left foreground is the establishment I knew as Matheos Brothers' soda fountain. Closer examination of this view taken from William Reed Gordon's 1963 book on this trolley line shows that the sign is advertising ICE CREAM. One of the storefronts down the tracks toward the trolley car was the early home of one of the first electric appliance dealers in Brockport. To the right and not visible on the opposite corner of State and Main (southeast corner) from the Strand Theatre is St. Luke's Episcopal Church. I attended my first Cub Scout meetings in their gym.

Long vertical cobwebs rose from the original Catholic Church's altar, reaching gracefully skyward. Those too were tracks that interested me. Silvery dust shimmered on them when the light in the nave was just right. My eyes were often riveted on that area above the altar. Dad had told me that the collection money went to heaven. After the ushers took the cash and envelopes back into the sacristy, I tried very hard to detect the collection's progress toward heaven. I never did see it, but never stopped looking.

It developed rather quickly that this, my first Catholic Church of many, was soon going to be the "old" church because a new one was to be built up on Main Street in the midst of Brockport's cluster of leading homesteads. I learned later that it was going to be built across from the Morgan home (my name for it; townspeople knew it as the Manning house) by then the home of the sister of Brockport's leading citizen, Gifford Morgan. That home was a large, well gabled, brick home built along Victorian lines. The dwelling lot was at the northeast corner of Main and South Street. The new Nativity of the Blessed Virgin Mary church would be built at the northwest corner of Main Street and Monroe Avenue. Monroe Avenue and South Street *almost* met at Main Street. These two central village edifices, the Catholic Church, and the home of the leading citizen of the village, would almost directly face each other across Main Street.

The new church construction was delayed a bit, first because there was a question about whether the property owners would ever be amenable to a sale that would lead to construction of a Catholic Church. It was probably acceptable to an earlier generation of townspeople when Father Michael Walsh, the founding pastor for the original church in 1851, decided to build his church down in the business section of town. He and his small band of parishioners chose a street that the builders of the trolley line in 1908 would decide was good for passenger traffic. The Sisters of St. Joseph located their first convent and school across Utica Street from that church on the southwest corner of Utica and Erie. Father Story was the first priest to have a long pastorate in Brockport. He and the Sisters of St. Joseph later located Brockport's eight grade brick school on a lot adjacent to the back of the old church bordering the northeast corner of Utica and Holley Street.

Though it caused some delay, the new church's property matter was finessed rather neatly. Dr. John Hazen, our family physician while I lived in Brockport, agreed to buy the property. Now, Dr. Hazen was not a Catholic and he was also not a bigot. He readily agreed to buy, and then to re-sell the property to the church. Its original wood dwelling, quite a nice home in its own right, would be used as a temporary Rectory. Father Krieg. Michael J. (for Joseph) Krieg became Nativity of the BVM's second pastor in 1917, having been assigned by the Diocese of Rochester as the permanent pastor after the death of Father Story. Father Krieg officiated at the wedding of my Mother and Dad in 1920. Father Story had passed away in 1914.

In 1925, Father Krieg began the process of pledges and mortgages to build the new church up on Main Street. I recall attending a ceremony in the temporary Rectory, an imposing family home, which was to be torn down to make way for the new church.

To be constructed of Ohio sandstone, the new church's cornerstone was laid in 1926 and its first Mass was celebrated in 1927. The next illustration shows the church with snow remnants receding and buds on the trees as the welcome sign of spring.

Illustration 5 -Church of the Nativity of the BVM

The stock market crash of the fall of 1929, the almost immediate failure of the Brockport State Bank of Commerce, and some terribly cold and snowy winters all hit Brockport in last years of a decade known as the Roaring Twenties.

The prosperity of 1926-1928 had been like an addict's high. Banks had so much money they begged the citizens to borrow. The stock market was going up, up, up.

My Dad borrowed on his family home and while operating the town's leading coal and produce business, was on the phone constantly to Rochester and his broker in the commodities market. Wheat, beans, barley, oats. Dad went broke before the crash of '29. So did others. Banks began to discover that the collateral for some mortgages would not cover the principal of the loan. Late one year, two carloads of cabbage showed up at the Dailey Coal and Produce Company on its Park Avenue siding on the New York Central Railroad. I asked Dad what he was going to do with the cabbage and why it arrived so late in the season. Dad said simply, "I got out of the market too late." A couple of years later, his brother Bill and nephew Murray built a sauerkraut plant in Albion, New York. The Dailey boys had learned something from father William.

Illustration Six is a photo of the original Dailey business in Brockport. The office in front was just across the tracks from Brockport's New York Central train station. This view looks east in the direction of Rochester.

Illustration 6 - Dailey Coal & Produce Company

Not pictured, either because it was out of the camera's view to the left or because it was not yet there, is a large cylindrical coal storage and delivery tank with chutes on its periphery controlling access to eight different sectors containing various kinds or grades of coal or coke. This tank would be filled using a conveyor parked next to and feeding from a railroad coal car. Although one sign advertises wood as a product, by my time in the twenties, wood was no longer a product.

In front of the office, platform scales and bins are revealed. These bins were used to offload coal if the load was overweight to the customer order (tons was the unit of measure). From these same bins, coal would be added to the load if the load were too light. Each vehicle had a "no load" weight so the customer received the difference between the loaded weight and the "no load" weight standard for that vehicle. A mix of trucks and wagons was used for a time. If a wagon was being used, the team of horses and the driver did not stand on the platform scales. When a truck was used, the driver got out during the weighing. By my time in visiting the office with Mother or Dad, the platform scales and small coal bins had been moved to the right side of the little office building and the building itself had a facing of sandstone and was a bit larger. Mother did some bookkeeping for the business and I would "play office," using the typewriter or a marvelous machine that embossed checks in red ink. After the last fire in the stalls, the low building on the left in the picture no longer existed. It is possible that this space was then used for the new coal tank.

The freight cars on the siding that went deepest into the property are shown alongside the grain elevators for unloading or loading. Produce was both a buy and sell proposition which the commodity markets simply mirrored. There were three deep grain bins in this elevator building and a sorting conveyor for apples or pears on its south side, the right side in this picture. The numerous wagons in this photo are full of cabbage. One sign advertises, "Buffalo Gluten Feed and Wheat Bran For Sale Here." That product was no longer handled in the twenties.

Beans and wheat used two shafts when I used to jump in them and the third held a crop of the season that might change season to season. Barley was handled before my time. Looking across the tracks northwest from the Dailey Coal and Produce office, one could see that behind the train station to the north was the Stull Lumber Company. Lumber companies always impressed me because they were so big and the wood smelled so good. Mr. Eugene Stull, a member of that family, became my history teacher and my favorite teacher in Brockport High School.

It was during this financial frenzy that Father Krieg built his new church. He could borrow without much resistance but still had to furnish collateral. What collateral could he offer but the ability of his parishioners to put money in the collection basket? He got the money to build his new church. It was built through two of the coldest winters recorded in Brockport. The facing coats of mortar, on the high inside vertical walls of the new church, were mottled with unsightly streaks left by the salt added to enable those walls to cure properly in the cold.

In an irony of the times, just three years after the new church was consecrated, there occurred a run on Brockport's only remaining bank, the First National Bank of Brockport. Father Krieg, by then not just a pillar of the church but a pillar of the town's financial community and holder of one of the largest bank mortgages, went down to the bank. He got up on a soapbox and gave the sermon of his life. The townspeople listened and the run on the bank was voluntarily terminated. The bank was saved for the time. Later, in President Roosevelt's 1933 bank moratorium, the bank did not reopen as such but the depositors in that later situation did not lose everything. Father Krieg was a leader and undertook many fine initiatives in the village.

While Father Krieg had many talents, he was not a man of great empathy. Even after the depression really set in, beginning in 1930 and 1931, he was still posting in the vestibule of the new church the names of those who were overdue on pew rent. That mortgage would be paid off.

I served many weekday morning Masses for Father Krieg. Making my way a mile through heavy unplowed winter snow was the easy part. Early Mass at 6: a.m. weekdays came a little before the horse-drawn sidewalk plows came by. Father was very demanding. The wine and water cruets were to be handed to him free of my fingers on their handles. The altar stairs were steep and the altar table loomed like a mountain plateau above my head. The lady who donated that brass Mass Book cradle with the lead bottom was not a young altar boy's friend. I prayed each day that I would have the strength to lift the Book to the altar when changing it from the Epistle to the Gospel side.

The lead altar boy would always kneel on the right on the lowest altar step. Father had a small, single mallet, five-tone xylophone in a mahogany box with a velvet lining. It was placed just to the right of the lead altar boy. A single announcement tone was to be struck at the beginning of the Eucharist, chime bar 2. The tones for the end of the Preface required more dexterity with the mallet on the chime bars, striking 1-2-3, 2-3-4, 3-4-5 in rapid order. This signified that the most solemn part of the Mass was about to begin. Another single tone was struck as the celebrant put his hands flat over the chalice to begin the solemn moment of the most solemn act. During the Consecration, the chime bars were struck in stately cadence, with chime bars 1-3-5 to be struck for the elevation of the host and chime bars 5-3-1 for the elevation of the chalice with wine. There were just five metal bars, one for each tone. Precision was required. If my fingers were to direct the mallet to the wrong tone for the specific Mass event, it would be distracting to everyone present.

One day my fingers betrayed me by wandering too close to those cruet handles as I was serving water and wine to Father at the Offertory. Father gave me a resounding slap across the face. My Dad later explained that Father Krieg had ulcers and the anticipation of his sacred duty with the altar wine made him grouchy. I accepted what Dad said and did not let it interfere with my relationship with the Church of the Nativity of the Blessed Virgin Mary. I was old enough, though, to sense that Dad was "reaching" for an explanation.

Attendance at early Mass on weekdays consisted of five or six ladies and no men. The ladies were very old and may have been praying for departed men. Some may have been thanking God for departed men. One lady who was always present, never missed. She wandered from place to place in the Church all during Mass .No one ever satisfied my curiosity about the lady. Direct experience with old age suggests that she had a senile dementia before that term gained recognition.

One relief, at least for an Altar Boy, to Father Krieg's severe demeanor came to us about 1928 or 1929. A very young Assistant Priest was sent to the Church of the Nativity of the Blessed Virgin Mary. I was assigned to serve Father Haughey's Christmas Day Masses. (I am in doubt about the spelling of his name. There were no church bulletins then. His name could well have been Hoye.) Father took the first scheduled Mass of Christmas Day at 7: a.m. and then celebrated two more Masses in quick succession. Thus, he fulfilled his obligation to celebrate three Masses on Christmas Day. My recollection is that the first Mass replete with Sermon, collection and so on took about 45 minutes and his next two Masses, unannounced schedule-wise, took about 15 minutes apiece. I served all three, alone, except for a few of the devout parishioners who would stay in church any time Mass was being celebrated. Father had to complete his obligation before commencement of Father Krieg's regular 9 a.m. Mass and he did. His Latin had a distinct Irish brogue to it, a sound I had not experienced before. It went well. The Irish voice, in English or in Latin, had a nice song quality that I enjoyed. After Mass, Father Haughey thanked me and gave me a dollar bill. I was astounded but not too shocked to keep it and thank him profusely. There was a man a boy could love.

Unfortunately for pupils and Altar Boys (and parishioners), Father Haughey's assignment came to an end quickly. He cracked a few jokes during his sermons and that was just too much for Father Krieg.

The next illustration is from the cover of a booklet published in 1961 by Franklin X. McCormick of Milwaukee, Wisconsin. The trio is in the Sacristy, and all wear a smile as they realize that one boy has on a cassock and surplice intended for a much smaller boy.

Illustration 7 - Altar Boys with Sister

Relative to the view from the pews, the Altar Boy changing room was to the right of the main Altar in our new church. To the left of the Altar was the Sacristy. The Sacristy was connected to the Rectory by a covered walkway. We wore the conventional black cassock with white surplice. We were required to have low, white tennis shoes with smooth soles. These were to be left on the floor of the closet in the changing room at all times and replaced with new ones when their whiteness wore off. When properly attired for Mass, we would join the Priest in the Sacristy by walking through a passageway behind the Altar.

Chapter Four - I Meet Sister Lucida

Domine, exaudi orationem meam.
Et clamor meus ad te veniat.

O Lord, hear my prayer.
And let my plea be heard.

I met Sister Lucida when I went to first grade in the early fall of 1926. Despite her nun's habit, all black and flowing except for a starched white bib on her chest and a starched white band in her headpiece, it was clear even to an urchin like me that she was young. And quite beautiful. I was five and one half years old.

The game of entering children into the "educational" process just as soon as an institution could be found that would take the child did not begin with later 20th century kindergartens, nursery schools and "pre-schools." Perhaps the World War II boomers and generation x-ers have pushed it a little further in order to support two parents working, but mothers and fathers before them were fully attuned to getting "precocious" Jane or Johnny off to school as soon as possible. I am witness to that.

Sister Lucida taught first and second grade in one of the four main classrooms of Nativity of the BVM school. With Sister Lucida, I experienced my first eclipse of the sun. She used a lighted candle to blacken small pieces of broken glass that she had persuaded us to bring to school. Thus "protected", we observed a solar eclipse in all of its majesty. The only other one I recall in any detail was in the movie, A Connecticut Yankee, when Will Rogers was able to win the day because the medieval soldiers discovered that he controlled light and darkness.

With Sister Lucida, I participated in my first grade Valentine's Day. Despite already demonstrated preferences, Sister saw to it that the less popular among us had plenty of Valentine cards. That took some doing because in the back row with the second graders sat a genial giant of a boy, or man. He was at least six feet tall when I first became aware of him. He was still sitting there, participating in second grade class activities, when I graduated six years later in 1932.

In the 1920s, first grade was the first association that a child had with school. It follows that the teacher of that first assembly of urchins makes an impression that coincides with the formation of early memory. There are so many firsts wrapped up in first grade. My time at the School of the Nativity of the Blessed Virgin Mary began in this rush of firsts. The front façade of the building in the illustration that comes next does much to reinforce my earliest memories. Happily for me, the building in this view has not changed from the day I first saw it.

Illustration 8 - School of the Nativity of the BVM

As I have noted, this building facing on Holley Street in Brockport was the second location for the school. Erected, according to its cornerstone in 1915, of bricks and mortar, it was still in 1926 a relatively new and impressive structure to a six-year old. There was a simple front entrance, used mostly by visitor dignitaries. I do not recall if the globe on the right hand lamp was missing when I attended school. This front entrance was in the center of a building that had a spacious center hall up a few steps from the doorway. Grades one and two were in the main room on the right and grades seven and eight were in an almost identical room on the left. A very small room immediately off the hall toward the Grade 7-8 room on the left as you entered the front door housed the library. That little room also contained the American Flag. There was a girl's lavatory and a boy's lavatory on this floor.

Proceeding up the center hall stairs led to the second floor center hall. The stairway to the second floor involved a complete turn so as one gained access to the second floor there was a main room on the left for the third and fourth grades, directly above the room on the first floor for first and second grades. To the right as one gained the second floor, was the room housing the fifth and sixth grades. This room was directly above the first floor room for seventh and eighth grades. The library and small utility closets on the first floor borrowed their space from the hall. Pupils entered the building through the center rear doors. The school buses with the "country kids" stopped on Utica Street opposite the rear entrance.

At the rear of each of the four main classrooms was a Cloak Room. A plain room with hangar hooks just above eye level all the way around except for the entrance on the right, this room exhaled strong odors, particularly in winter as the snow melted into the clothes and the steam heat added to the humid air. The Cloak Room was the scene of a memorable encounter with Sister Florentia when I was in the fifth grade. We'll come to that in a later chapter. Each classroom had a rostrum in the center against the back wall and on this elevated structure, Sister's desk was perched. There were blackboards on two sides of the rooms. Each student's seat held the desk of the student behind. There were inkwells depressed into the desktop on the forward right side of each desk. Left handers were not encouraged. I throw right-handed and bat a ball left-handed. Sister saw to it that wherever there might be a left-handed tendency the pupil was encouraged to be right-handed. Most decisions were shaped by the facility constraints. My tenure of six years in the School of the Nativity of the BVM was the result of crowded classrooms. We took Palmer Method writing from brown covered booklets. I never saw a Palmer Method writing booklet in which the cursive characters were shaped for a left-handed person.

At age 5 1/2 for first grade in September 1926, and with western New York's harsh winter coming, Dad drove me to school every morning that first fall term. He let me walk home, a distance of slightly over one mile. On those mornings, he always stopped and took me into the school, and he always stopped to talk with Sister

Lucida. They talked about Sister Mary Joseph who had been Dad's first teacher in that same school, though in an earlier building, a generation before me.

You see, Dad grew up in his family home on South Avenue in Brockport, with his seven brothers and one sister. That was a large Victorian home with an addition built off the back when it became populated with so many Dailey boys. That home had a slate roof and redwood siding. The barn out back was of the same construction, and featured stalls for the horses and even an icehouse with thick sawdust walls. There was a well for drinking water in the back yard and a rainwater cistern in the basement. It was to this home at 48 South Avenue in Brockport that Dad and Mother brought me from an apartment in Rochester when I was ten months old at the end of 1921. As the youngest of the Dailey boys, my Dad inherited his family home along with Brockport's Dailey Coal and Produce Company, the hometown-based business of his father. Dad's surviving brothers had earlier taken over Grandfather Dailey business interests in Albion, New York, Morton New York, Oakfield New York and Kendall, New York.

I know that Dad loved the School of the BVM, and I know he loved to talk about Sister Mary Joseph who was still there in my first year in 1926 as a sort of elder statesman. Still, the thought came to me in later years that if I could walk home, I could walk to school. For all but that first half year, I did walk both ways. Dad was becoming an alcoholic though I had little awareness of it then. He was not entirely reliable in his self appointed duty of driving me to school in that first half year.

Sober, my father was a very entertaining Irishman with many stories. It occurred to me in later years that he liked talking with Sister Lucida and she enjoyed talking with him. These are thoughts that filter through to a person later on. Some of the puzzling aspects of childhood disappear when you figure them out.

Though I would not see Sister Emma as a teacher until I made it into her room on the floor above Sister Lucida's room, for grades three and four, I made her acquaintance during grade one because she taught us the Latin for serving Mass. I learned the Mass Latin on the back stoop of the convent which had been re-located to a frame house on Monroe Avenue next to the new Rectory. The new Rectory was built of the same material as the new church and connected with it by a covered walkway. While I made my First Confession and First Holy Communion in the "old" church, where I was duly informed that the Sacred Host might taste like peanut butter, I served my first 6 a.m. daily Mass in the new church.

Trips that took the place of a day of classes were major events. Each sister took her turn shepherding the flock for these pilgrimages. Sister Lucida was our tour guide for the second grade's trip in 1927 to St. Bernard's Seminary in Rochester, New York. This was an early summer trip, just before school let out. I will never forget the statues and the Stations of the Cross in grottoes along narrow pathways chipped out of the Genesee River gorge.

Rivers are like magnets to children. I have the feeling that a comparable trip for eight-year olds would be ruled out in this new Millennium, even if St. Bernard's still existed. For that trip in 1927, we had a young adult assigned to each of us but the riverbank was very steep and a fall was but a step or two away. For those readers fortunate enough to have seen some of this country's great rivers, like the Mississippi, the Hudson, and the Connecticut, the Genesee River (like the Niagara River just a few miles to the west) flows the wrong way. The Genesee originates in Pennsylvania's Allegheny Mountains and flows about 158 miles *north* into Lake Ontario.

It happened rarely. I never anticipated when it might happen. But I learned that there was some emotional moment in the teaching life of every sister where she might break into tears. Most often, this situation developed when one of us boy monsters would initiate some wildly hilarious course of action intended to bring an end to all decorum. I never encountered a boy who could persist in such errant activity in the face of a sister driven to tears. Crying, I learned early, had functions other than an evidence of weakness.

The last occasion in which I was in the presence of Sister Lucida was the 100th anniversary celebration for the founding of the School of the Nativity of the BVM. It was a warm, brief, encounter in May of 1976. I have a profound regard for the mother of Jesus, and I hope she'll forgive me for the abbreviation, BVM.

Chapter Five - The Raleighs

Orate, fratres, ut meam ac vestrum sacrificium acceptible fiat apud Deum Patrem omnipotentem.
Suscipiat Dominus sacrificium de manibus tuis, ad laudem et gloriam nominis sui, ad utilitatem quoque nostram, totiusque ecclesiae suae sanctae.

Brethren, pray that my sacrifice and yours may be acceptable to God the Father almighty.
May the Lord receive the sacrifice from your hands to the praise and glory of his Holy Name, for our welfare and that of all His Holy Church.

The Latin passage above, beginning with the word "Suscipiat", was, except for the Confiteor, the longest passage an Altar Boy had to know by heart. We learned it so well that it intruded on my recitation of the passage in English for many years after Vatican II. The opening phrase can also be translated, "Pray, brothers..." That phrase is relevant to the brotherhood I experienced in the presence of the family this story now reveals.

It would be no surprise to a reader to discover that a small boy might tarry along the way to school or on his way home. The urge to pause became overpowering when an erstwhile pupil encountered a huge steam locomotive astride the railroad-bridge over the street on which he was making his way to school. Especially if that locomotive was taking on water or coal, and hissing steam at intervals. Almost always, there was an engineer

61

or fireman that would wave to you. That street was Utica Street at a point almost half way between my home and the Parochial School. But, there was another attraction just two doors down South Avenue from my home and it was the home of the Raleigh family. We lived between the Fosters on the west and the Caswells on the east. Mr. Foster worked at the A&P canning factory and Mr. Caswell owned one of the town's insurance agencies. The Fosters had a parrot whose summers were spent on their front porch. My mother would call me from the back farm lots in her soprano voice, "Frank-eeee." That parrot learned a perfect imitation of her call to me. I made many trips back home, only to discover that Mother had not called me at all.

On leaving my house for school, and after passing the Fosters on my way westward toward Main Street, I came past the home of the Charles Raleigh family.

The Raleigh home stood on the brow of South Avenue's hill that led west and downward toward Main Street. That hill provided many important sledding and biking events. Kid-developed events, of course. I don't want the word "events" to get the reader thinking anything more than glorious abandon in local fun.

The Raleigh home was unspectacular, with its narrow front defined by a simple inverted V roof and a strictly utilitarian front door on the right. When you stepped inside that doorway, you were in the front living room. There was no hallway unless you called the stairs leading directly to the second floor a hall of sorts. But then, you never went in that door anyway. Only the occasional door to door salesman or precious metals buyer or organ grinder with monkey would even think of knocking on that front door. The house kind of expanded as you went toward the back. Behind the living room, there was a dining room on the right with a small sewing room off to the left. Then one got to the main room of the house, the kitchen with its wood range at the left rear left. In front of the stove was a large oval kitchen table, long axis front to back, always covered with tablecloth and always holding essentials like salt and pepper, and sugar bowl. There was usually a leftover coffee cup on the table. Most business, and almost all social events took place at that table. Behind the kitchen was a back kitchen of almost the same size, with every imaginable tool not currently in active use waiting and hoping for at least one last recall.

The back kitchen was home to rifles, shotguns, kerosene lamps, hurricane lamps, assorted tubs, cooking trays, grinders, saws and wrenches of every imaginable shape, hammers, nails, discarded weighing scales, every conceivable mind stimulator that heaven might set before a small boy. Every space was occupied. The impact was metal, almost all of it dark. There were no shiny stainless steel items, though there were a few metal pieces with shiny, crumbling chrome coatings. The gun barrels showed evidence of being treated with fresh coats of oil but the lasting impression of most of the articles was dark metal, a lot of it rusting. Nothing was ever thrown away. To this day, I have little desire to go to museums. How could a museum offer the flood of dreams stimulated by the Raleigh's 1927 back kitchen?

Family access to the house was through the back kitchen. Customer access was through the side door leading into the store. My own access was privileged, it seemed to me, for I could and did use the latter two entrances depending on my purpose. I am sure now, putting some refreshed thoughts together, that there were times when I may have been tolerated, but I always took my entrance to the Raleigh home as a privilege, enhanced by a sense of positive anticipation.

As I have related, directly off the kitchen on the west side of the house was an addition that served as a small convenience store. But the mental vision of today's 7-11 does not serve to give the reader a sight, sound and smell appreciation for Kitty Raleigh's store. That store entrance consisted of a well worn set of stairs and plain door and was completely unremarkable. There was no hint that a store existed behind the door. I am sure that bread was the principal sales item. Bond Bread and Buttercrust Bread were the standards. Toward the end of my life in Brockport, which was pretty well over by 1935, Wonder Bread was added, possibly because Hostess cup cakes from the same baker had developed a following. There were cookies, National Biscuit style, in rectangular front cardboard boxes with glass closures. One would open the glass and sometimes with a scoop or dispensed paper cover for the hand, remove a number of fig newtons or raisin tea biscuits for Mrs. Raleigh, who would then weigh them, brown bag them, and tell you what you owed. In packaged goods, Educator crackers were a favorite of mine. A glassed in counter top held green (spearmint) leaves and nigger babies and sweet concoctions shaped like little bananas. Nigger babies were the product name of the twenties for a licorice-based, sugared, candy product in the shape of a baby. There were no black persons in Brockport. The darkest complexions I can recall were on the Gallos, a wonderful Italian family living on the west side of town. "Pete" Gallo was a friend of mine through the middle grades of Parochial School. Though I was never much of a gum chewer, Mrs. Raleigh carried Wrigley and Beech-Nut gum, and bubble gum with a forgettable brand name. The Mars Corporation family included Milky Way, then Snickers and finally for the sugar addict who had economic problems and needed more for the money, Mars introduced the Three Musketeers. Hershey was well represented with an almond bar and a flat bar of chocolate squares. Nestle's products were not then a regular counter feature.

I had an almost fatal weakness for National Biscuit Company fig newtons. I often needed to ponder the events of life early in the morning, I would ring the store bell and Mrs. Raleigh would have to set down her morning cup of Postum in her kitchen so that I could buy a pound of fig newtons. This sequence would often end by my climbing to the top of the Beech tree next to my house to eat the pound in one tree sitting. It was also important to me that the Raleigh's store carried a few boxes of choice cigars in addition to all the leading brands of cigarettes. Some cigar boxes (I remember Bold Cigars, 3 for 10-cents, Dutch Masters and La Palinas) came with glass tops so you could see what you were buying. Mrs. Raleigh or husband Charlie would occasionally give me one of those glass cigar box covers when I needed to make or replace a window in my hut.

Father Charlie was a chauffeur, gardener and general aide de camp to the well-to-do Cleveland family who lived at the corner of Adams Street and Kenyon Street. Mother "Kit" Raleigh baked irresistible wonders in her kitchen. And sent over the basics of a good meal to our house when things were going bad there and she knew Sis and I were home alone. Kit Raleigh did not bake delicacies because Kit did not go for finger cookies and the like. She baked delectable items like big black strap molasses cookies of a kind I have never seen since. That is one recipe I would die for today. Kitty never tired of cooking as long as Charlie would "get the wood in." She did have a modern electric toaster and while the cookies or pies or roasts or whatevers were cooking, she would feed me toast with butter and homemade jam. One morning I ate 31 pieces of toast. At about slice twenty-five many had gathered and pronounced it the all time record. But, when a cookie showed up, I could still handle it.

Daughter Rose Raleigh worked in a flower shop and greenhouse down on West Street, the main road to Holley. When Rose, with the counsel and commitment of help from all the family, decided she could do the whole thing right behind her home on South Avenue, another of the endless stream of Raleigh enterprises was created. Rose was also an attractively plump soprano. One momentous day, the Raleighs and as many neighbors as could be wedged into their home, gathered with ears straining to hear an old battery powered tuned

RF radio. The station was WHAM, Rochester's pioneer AM radio station. Rose was making her radio debut. Her voice rose in majestic opening notes, accompanied by piano. Then, in mid aria, silence. With no explanation, a few minutes later an entirely different program began. Rose was gone. When she returned to Brockport, Rose reported that ASCAP, the license holder of the song, had stopped the presentation because no one had paid the fees due the song's publisher. Actually, someone employed by WHAM stopped the rendering when the song did not turn up on a permissions list. I never heard Rose sing again.

Henry was Rose's betrothed. He was Henry Schmidt, a taciturn man of several enterprises that took him on the road occasionally. He and Rose never seemed to get married but this was a family that accepted you for your enterprise and your steadfastness.

Chubby Raleigh, Charles Jr. to be more specific, but the nickname Chubby was appropriate, occasionally filled in for Charlie Sr. at chauffeuring, but mostly was in business with Henry as a owner-distributor for slot machines. Chub had a girlfriend who was not a live-in girl friend but came to visit frequently. Well, frequently enough so that I could keep track. Like Henry with Rose, Chub's romance was a longstanding affair that never resulted in marriage during my young life in town. Some weeks, Chubby's ladyfriend would not put in an appearance. I figured out they were having a little spat. Then one day she would come and all was well again. Spats came and went in that kitchen and laughter did too. I said there was a sewing room off the dining room on the east side. That room could also be accessed from the kitchen and doubled as an office and study and a place to listen to that battery powered tuned RF radio receiver. Later the heterodyne radio receivers came in with far better tuning, more volume and less static and no more batteries. The Raleighs always bought the latest and best in anything of a utility nature. I was fond of their Atwater Kent and the show, Amos and Andy, just around supper time. The dialogue was funny and the fact that it came at meal time doubled its attraction for me.

One of the distractions to a boy wending his way to school might be an early morning decision by Chub and Henry to clean out the garage. This garage had a flat roof with a slight slope to the back wall, a dirt floor, a somewhat sagging wall on its west side, and was wide enough for about three vehicles. It contained at any one time a few slot machines awaiting repair or relocation, some farm implements like a small motorized plow or trencher, a car or a pick up truck The whole was quite porous to nature. Cleaning it out meant killing a few rats. This was accomplished by putting down a few slices of bread, getting sundry chairs out in the driveway for shooters or spectators, and loading one or more rifles or shotguns from the back kitchen. And then waiting. I was always optimistic that Sister would understand.

Not to forget Helen, the youngest Raleigh, and younger sister to Rose. When I got in trouble for overstaying my welcome at the Raleighs, Helen would be my advocate, to my parents or hers. She was a teenager, about eighteen when I first thought about how old people were. When I was younger and "stayed over" because my parents were not home, it was in Helen's bed that I would first go to sleep and then someone would move me to a spare bed when Helen came upstairs for the night. Helen had a feather mattress that did not help my hay fever, but it sure was comfortable. Helen became a hairdresser, and later got married and moved to a nearby town. When Helen was learning hairdressing, I was the "practice" head of hair for her. That early "set" material did not like to give up so I often went around with kind of an ocean wave hairdo, the hair tending to stand up. Nobody ever mentioned it and it did not bother me. Helen was my friend. Helen's baby sitter chores with me were broken up when she might have to assist her mother with meal preparation. For about 30 minutes, Charlie would take me to the "radio room" and we would listen together to Lowell Thomas and Amos and Andy. Lowell Thomas had the widest listening audience of radio news. The Amos and Andy show was the premier situation comedy of radio days. Those radio programs were 15 minutes each. While Mr. Raleigh, the name by which I addressed him, shared these programs with me, he wanted no distractions during this period of his early evening. He wanted to hear every word. Consequently, I could for years after repeat back many phrases from situations in the Amos and Andy show.

The Raleighs were industrious, to make a great understatement. They would try anything that had the potential for a successful small business. In the late fall, there was always the preemptive requirement to get Mr.

Cleveland's Packard ready for the annual trip to Florida for the months of Brockport's severe winters. The Clevelands, Milo and Catherine, had two children, Sybil and Merritt. I caddied for Sybil at the Churchville, New York pubic golf course. I kept score and if I could shave a few strokes from Sybil's score, there always seemed to be a boost in the caddy fee. Two other caddy customers were the Tullochs, father and son. They managed the men's clothing department at Sibley, Lindsay and Curr Company, a Rochester department store. They were Scotsmen and excellent golfers. They were extremely fussy about a lost ball. My long vision was excellent and we never lost a ball. At the 9th hole, they bought me lunch and then proceeded to play another nine holes. I carried two bags, which, after biking from Brockport to Churchville did get a little heavy on the back nine. They were great tippers so my theory that the Scots were thrifty about lost balls did not hold up. Years later it dawned on me that they were competing with each other, were scrupulous in counting strokes, and neither wanted a stroke penalty for a lost ball.

Milo Cleveland's sister married my Uncle Oz, making her my Aunt Florence. She was a beautiful woman, wonderful to me, and lived to be 100, outliving her husband, my father's brother Oswald, by 60 years. All the Clevelands were good looking. Merritt dated movie star Claire Trevor from Hollywood. Sybil married a well known Rochester man named Beach. Depending on how many of the Cleveland family went in their car for the trip south, would determine how many Raleighs would go along. Kit rarely went, having her store and baking business to tend to. But the rest all made a trip or two. Loaded into their car for the return trip were exotic seashells. These were large shells. The closely pressed ear could detect gentle Gulf sea breeze sounds.

New projects would generally be started in the spring when Charlie senior would have completed his winter sojourn with the Clevelands.

If you are wondering, family head Milo Cleveland made his money as a road builder. One road familiar to us in Brockport was the Million-Dollar Highway, a section of NY State Route 31 that joined Brockport, Spencerport, and Rochester. Something went wrong in Spencerport. The road had a little detour, a hook with a sharp right turn followed by a sharp left turn as one proceeded toward Rochester. Possibly some farmer would not sell a lot or two and the road builders did the best they could. One possible suspect in my farm holdout theory owned an unpainted barn on which emblazoned in large yellow letters, " Chew Mail Pouch Tobacco" on one line, followed by a line which read "Treat Yourself To The Best." Possibly that barn and its advertisement made up the impediment that led to the crook in the new highway. When we went to Rochester for a Sunday movie and dinner, this barn at the slow down curve in Spencerport, conveyed words that stayed with me for life. The Million-Dollar Highway was an east-west alternative to the Ridge Road, also known as the Honeymoon Trail, closer to Lake Ontario. Marked State Route 104, that trail, by my time there a paved road, went east to Rochester via Greece and west to

Niagara Falls and Lewiston, New York. Route 31 and one of its alphabetical alternate roads, like 31F and so on, also went west to Niagara Falls or Buffalo but Route 31 took a frequently interrupted route along the Niagara escarpment whereas the Ridge Road was relatively level along a lower and gentler ridge above Lake Ontario. Some publicist for Niagara Falls painted a pair of red hearts pierced by the usual arrow, on the east side of all the south-side telephone poles, visible to west bound travelers.

Charlie helped Rose build her greenhouse to compete with her former employer. Charlie helped Helen create her little hair salon. Charlie helped Chubby and Henry with their slots and other enterprises. Charlie built an outdoor miniature golf course on a small portion of the five-acre field he owned behind his house and welcomed paying customers for that very brief fad. That lot usually had a tomato crop or corn crop, with the local A&P canning factory as the customer and processor. Some years, an alfalfa crop would break up the sequence and renew the soil. Charlie had an old Fordson tractor, which when not in use was usually parked next to a rock pile in the middle of the field. Like many farmers, Charlie let it stay there all winter. And, as with many farms when the elders became too old for crop harvesting, the Fordson reached its final resting place next to that rock pile when I left town in 1935.

Raleigh's meadow was the starting point for pheasant hunts in the fall. I would be allowed to tag along on special days to watch the hunters use their hunting dogs to point, or set, and flush the birds which would usually fall with one shot. Later there was conversation with Kit Raleigh, with the hunters using phrases like "quite a bit of shot in this one, Kit." I learned the advantages of double-barreled shotguns, and the differences between 12 gauge and 20 gauge. Mr. Raleigh and his group of hunters never allowed me to shoot. Since my Dad would not let me have a rifle, I did not ever fire a gun with powder cartridges until I was introduced to a Navy Lieutenant named Mumma, his rifle range, and the "thirty ought six" at the U.S. Naval Academy in the summer of 1939. I have never fired a shotgun.

There was no apparent central thrust to the Raleigh enterprises. This loving family was happy to survive, to have a few of the good things of life, and to do wonderful things for their neighbors. The wealth of the Milo Cleveland family provided Charlie Raleigh with occasional employment and some memorable trips to Florida. Most of all, Charlie Raleigh enjoyed a sense of contribution of his diverse skills wherever these were needed. This was blue collar work with the joys of independence. The Raleighs were a family devoid of envy.

The Dailey family had its share of entrepreneurs too. Grandfather William was the son of a farmer and became a produce dealer. His son John F. Dailey invested in an invention that would teach a person how to drive a golf ball. Two of his sons, John F. Jr. and Murray, became New York State Amateur Golf champions. Uncle John also invested in a three-wheeled car. Unsuccessful. He owned a liquor store across from Shea's Buffalo theatre on Main Street in Buffalo New

York and next to that store he operated an orange juice dairy where the juice was squeezed in a contraption that passersby could watch in the store window. The juice dairy also offered good sandwiches. When cousin Tommy Dailey and I attended Niagara University some years later, hunger pains made it worth thumbing to Buffalo to get the juice and sandwich combo, courtesy of Uncle John. A gracious provider and a man who understood boys, John F. Dailey later opened another liquor store in Rochester, New York. My Uncle Bill, William G. Dailey, owned a thriving produce business in Albion, New York. He and Uncle John, as entrepreneurs, most closely followed their father, with their interest in the transfer of goods that one could touch as they passed from one owner to another.

My Dad and his brother Oz, Jesse Oswald Dailey, invested in and operated an indoor miniature golf course in downtown Brockport during that craze of the early thirties. Fifty rusting putters in our basement were a reminder to me that fads come fast and go fast. Though Dad took over operation of the original family coal and produce business, he was always involved in the commodity markets where he bought and sold goods that he never physically touched. Dad spent his final thirty plus years as a customer's man in brokerage offices. Uncle Don became Vice President of the Genesee Brewing Co. in Rochester, after duties as Rochester, New York's Commissioner of Public Safety, a senior position in public relations with the Eastman Kodak Co, and a few years as Postmaster of the city of Rochester. Uncle Don also put in some time in brokerage companies. Uncle Vin, Vincent Dailey, worked for Jim Farley, who was Chairman of the Democratic Party in New York State and succeeded to that job himself when Farley became Chairman of the national Democratic Party and Postmaster General in the first two Roosevelt administrations. While all of these Dailey boys departed from working the soil that supported their Irish grandfather, and followed their own father in that respect, only the older brothers retained their father's pursuit of direct business ownership. Politics and merchant relationships became the forte of the younger brothers. The sons and their one sister were born over a span of 20 years, and the changing natures of their breadwinning pursuits were reflective of our country's changes.

One main distinction of the Raleighs from the Daileys in enterprise was that the Raleighs did it without borrowing money. Each of their businesses was built with seed money from the effort that came before it. The Daileys were more accustomed to borrowing and sometimes it got them into trouble.

That generation before me, my father, his brothers and sister, would be worthy of more examination than I can attend to here. College at Georgetown was underwritten for most of the boys. My Dad's suitcase is full of artifacts and testimonials and photos relating to academic (valedictorian), sport and religious achievement at Georgetown Prep. Why he only lasted a year and one half at Georgetown University remains mostly a mystery to me. He talked about dental appointments as a way of skipping classes. But, I believe alcohol had become a factor. While all the Dailey boys had their bouts with alcohol, only my Dad and Uncle Oz failed to shake it before it permanently marred their life. Uncle Oz died in St. Mary's Hospital in Rochester from choking on his own vomit. He had been given a sedative after a binge and then no one checked on him before he was discovered dead. My father lost his marriage before he found Alcoholics Anonymous. These were the two youngest in the large family and the two who were closest together in friendship. Both were of draft age for World War I. Both saw two brothers, a sister, their Dad and Mother die in a period of just three years. Both began adulthood with the benefit of economic sufficiency that their father had earned. They were warm and generous men. Dad put hundreds of his customers "on the cuff" for coal during brutal winters in the late twenties. Coal was a life-sustaining requirement in Brockport's winters.

Those were long winters. Parties sustained the social set for some of the long nights. The Episcopal Church initiated a fund raising bridge tournament that used up one night a week for the 20 hardest weeks of at least two winters that I can recall.

Bridge was the "rage" of the late twenties and thirties. First came Auction Bridge. Our home had books by George Ade that explained how to play the game. Then, the ultimate bridge game, Contract Bridge, obsoleted all forms of the game before it. The name of Ely Culberson appeared on instruction booklets found in every living room. A third stage, Duplicate Contract Bridge, had not yet arrived when Father Veazey of St.Luke's decided he could generate a little badly needed income for his Church and give the townspeople something to do all winter. Dad and Uncle Oz entered the first 20-week contest as partners. At the end of the tournament Dad and Uncle Oz, both good card players, had won. There developed some murmuring from the other two-person teams. One statistic that came forth was that Dad and Uncle Oz had only played together three times during the 20 evenings of the tournament. Their drinking binges did not match so the one available simply picked up a substitute and played. One week both were unavailable so they forfeited all score for that week, yet still were point leaders at the conclusion of the tournament. I believe two prizes were finally awarded, one to Dad and Uncle Oz, and one to the highest performing team that had played together and stayed together.

Let me skip forward from early youth to relate an entrepreneurial event that occurred many years later. While working for a graphics company in South Hadley, Massachusetts, I was sent to Rochester to consult with Haloid-Xerox about a potential cooperative engineering project. I took a room at the Treadway Inn located at the corner of East Avenue and Alexander Street. The bell man seemed a bit old for that kind active duty but he was very helpful and I had quite a bit of baggage related to the upcoming discussions. As we were walking down the hall, I ventured a question about a Rochester hotel well known to me from my youth. I asked, "Is the Seneca Hotel still operating?" "No" he answered, "It has been torn down as part of a revival project for downtown Rochester." Then he added, "I worked there for many years." "Oh", I said, "My Dad lived there for a number of years. His name is Frank Dailey."

"Well, do I ever know Frank Dailey. We were in business at the Seneca for quite awhile." My curiosity was aroused as Rochester's familiarity was being revived. "What business was that?" I asked. "Your Dad had a brother here who owned a liquor store. Frank would buy liquor from his brother by the case and keep it in his room. When I received a call from a hotel guest to get a bottle of liquor, instead of going to the Seneca bar, I would go to your Dad's room and get a bottle. We split the profits." His warmly intended story had begun to move toward touchy ground. I was being updated on the liquor matter. "Yes", the bell man went on, "we made a lot of money. But one night when I went to Frank's room, only one case remained and it was down to seven bottles. As I took the seventh bottle, Frank informed me that we were now out of business. I asked him what had gone wrong. He told me that the six remaining bottles were just 'too good to sell'."

In Brockport, I was something of an entrepreneur myself. I mowed our lawn for free, A.V. Fowler's lawn across the street for $1.00, and the Engel's lawn up the street past the Caswell's also for a dollar. Mr. Engel ran the town's jewelry store. The Fowler home was new. One of my own carpenter supply opportunities came when Mr. Fowler tore down the original home and built a modern one on the site. For awhile, nails and wood were plentiful. From the Fowler's original home and garage, I recall that only Vinnie Fowler's homing pigeons and their roost survived. The landscaping involved new sod and that meant the new grass cut easily. While it was a large lawn, it was an easy dollar. The Engel's lawn was quite another story. While the lot was small, the entire back was wire grass. My Dad's hand mower, even when sharpened, was no match for that grass. That dollar was hard earned. In the winter I shoveled sidewalks, even though the town sent around a horse drawn sidewalk snowplow for the public streets. A lot of the men had to get out earlier and the town plow would not touch driveways and the walk leading to the dwelling door. I usually did about four walks before going to school unless I was the Altar Boy for six a.m. Mass for the particular week. Mr. Lancashire, at the corner of Main Street and Centennial Avenue had a long length of walk because his home was on the corner. But, he paid generously and I never forgot generosity.

I also sold Crowell Publishing Company publications, Colliers, a weekly, Woman's Home Companion a bi-weekly and the American Magazine, a monthly. For each five cent Colliers magazine I received 1 1/2 cents, for each Woman's Home Companion at a dime I received 4 cents, and for each 25 cent American Magazine, I received 6 cents. It did not take a kid long to figure that the 4 cents on a 10 cent sale was the one to push. Besides, Colliers, the bigger seller in the Crowell line at 5 cents, was up against the Saturday Evening Post. I usually read some of the Colliers' stories before making my rounds. This was door to door selling, one afternoon each week. I found out later that I was not as sharp a businessman as my

Dad. The Birdsall twins grew up across the street on South Avenue when my Dad was growing up. I discovered when I visited Edgar and Judy Birdsall years later when they lived in California, that my Dad got ten dollars from his father for cutting our South Avenue lawn. Dad then farmed the job out to the Birdsall twins for five dollars, pocketing the other five. I tried hard to get Pete Scripture's route delivering the Rochester Times Union every afternoon except Sunday. I walked the route with Pete many times in anticipation of his retirement but he never retired.

We began this chapter with challenges to a boy's progress as he made his way to school. In the very late spring, just before the interruption in education known as summer, at the Brockport Normal School ground on Utica Street, there gathered a collection of large tents and tent poles. By the time I would be making my way home, these tents would be erected in orderly rows, their backs to the railroad tracks. After a day or two of observing these preparations, I became informed that an event known as Chautauqua had arrived in our village. With the possible exception of Decoration Day, this became a crowning event of one span of my young life. Chautauqua lasted several days and in my free time, I fully indulged in its offerings. The week often extended into my summer vacation, so that I could spend all day taking in the lectures in the various tents. And varied these talks were. The Christian religion was emphasized in many tents although the variations from tent to tent of the "message" given in these tents were a little too subtle for a wide-eyed boy. Other tents had a definite business overtone, again with a Christian flavor. Still other tents featured the arts, particularly music. I received an introduction to "seating" on these grounds. I discovered that seating could be rented for occasions, a myriad of oak folding chairs, and that the funeral parlors provided such service. For me, the ultimate pleasure of Chautauqua came as the affair neared its end. Vendors with ice cream in cylindrical cardboard containers did not want to take the depleted containers back to the factory so they began to discount their cones. I learned that if I waited till the very end, the discount would result in free cones. Bartholomay's chocolate cones, now double dippers and free, overrode all my urges to try many other fine flavors.

Brockport's Drug Stores, as these were called before the words "pharmacy", or in some cities with European influences, "chemists," came into general use, were also examples of entrepreneurship. There were two, Dobson's, The Rexall Store, and Simmon's, which was marked by its neatness and display of a chemist's mortar and pestle. I knew what these tools were by sight, having examined them in many visits to Mr. Simmon's store. But for those who have not seen them, American Heritage Dictionary informs us that a pestle is a club shaped hand tool for grinding or mashing substances in a mortar. That leaves us with the mortar. It looked like a coffee mug. While Dobson's had a soda fountain, and was important to me for its ice cream cone dipped in warm, liquid chocolate, our family actually knew the Simmons family socially.

My mother played tennis doubles with Dotty Simmons, and tennis singles against that same lady. She was Ed Simmon's wife. A doubles trophy is still in our family, having been earned in a tournament organized by the social set and played on one of Milo Cleveland's clay courts on Allen Street.

Ed Simmons was a wonderful, kindly man, with a good sense of humor. He had a cherubic face and would open the store at night if a town doctor had a patient needing relief that drugs could provide. That of course included those with the disease of alcoholism. One of the oft-prescribed drugs for getting over a hangover was sodium amatol. It would let you sleep.

One time Ed himself got sick. Really sick and not alcohol for he rarely touched the stuff. For reasons never made clear, on this occasion he prescribed for himself. Perhaps he could not reach a doctor or perhaps he just felt confident. By then, my father's dosage was up to 5-grain sodium amatols, taken perhaps two at a time every four hours. Do not hold me to the exact amount. Its absence will not detract from the story. Ed decided that my father's dosage would be OK to take himself. The only problem was that Dad, a regular two week binge drinker, had built up a tolerance to sodium amatol. So, Mr. Simmons took Dad's dosage. Ed slept for four days. There was some concern but when he awoke, his misery had left him.

Chapter Six - Sister Emma

Memento etiam, Domine, famulorum famularumque tuarum, Sister Emma, Sister Florentia, et Sister Lucida, qui nos praecesserunt cum signo fidei, et dormiunt in somno pacis.

Remember also, O Lord, your servants Sister Emma, Sister Florentia, and Sister Lucida, who have gone before us with the sign of faith, and rest in the sleep of peace.

The passage above is part of the Celebrant's remembrance for the dead in the last part of the Eucharistic Prayer after the Consecration. It was not part of the Altar Boy's recitation.

I was reintroduced to Sister Emma for my third grade year in her grades three and four room on the second floor directly over the first and second grade room in which I had first come to the school with Sister Lucida as the teacher. I had first met with Sister Emma more than a year earlier on the back stoop of the Sister's Convent on Monroe Avenue. That Convent was just behind the new Rectory. It was the summer of 1927. There, usually in bright sunlight, Sister Emma taught me my Latin and then taught me the procedure for using it as an Altar Boy.

My earliest recalled summers were filled with many activities, rarely organized. One organized duty for me was to go to Doctor Hazen's office three afternoons a week, Mondays, Wednesdays and Fridays, from May until August 15. There I was given a hypodermic needle full of an experimental serum extract that the State of New York was testing for hay fever and asthma. It came in a small vial with a brown rubber top. It was kept in the refrigerator. When I arrived, Dr. Hazen's sister, who was his receptionist, signed me in. I usually did not have to wait long. Dr. Hazen took me into his Pharmacy, removed the serum vial from his refrigerator, plunged the hypo into its rubber top and withdrew the prescribed amount, took my upper arm and pushed the needle into it and depressed the plunger. He then swabbed the spot a second time with an alcohol filled cotton ball, having done this before administering the "shot" as well. He then poured into my hand some "sugar pills." May was chosen to start the series because of "rose fever" and August 15 was the ripening date for ragweed, my principal tormentor. No need for shots after that date. The fat was in the fire and the shots had either done their work or had failed. With me, they worked. Occasionally, Doctor John Livermore Hazen left the office, and his waiting patients, in a hurry. This was because he was on call for trolley line accidents. Let me quote Mr. William Reed Gordon's fascinating book on Brockport's trolley service, page 82.

"Motorman M. Harris stopped his trolley at Youngs siding 16 (near Brockport) one afternoon and waited for his conductor to open the switch so he could run in on the siding as he was scheduled to meet an eastbound passenger car at this point. While the conductor was unlocking the switch, Harris looked up the track and saw the eastbound trolley coming at him at high speed. He yelled to his conductor to run, opened his cab door and jumped. After the crash, the front of his trolley was demolished, he found his stool had the four legs broken off, and later he found the back of the stool about seventy feet from the car along the right-of-way. No one was killed, but the passengers were somewhat shaken up. The other motorman had also jumped, when he realized there was going to be a 'corn field meet', as railroad men named these unexpected collisions."

One story in which a passenger got off the trolley too soon (fatally, it developed), ended with the conductor reporting, "...so I went back into the car and when we pulled into Brockport, I notified Dr. Hazen, called up the dispatcher and told him about the accident, and then we went on to Rochester."

Doctor Hazen participated in one of the village's great dramas. His own son, John Jr., called Johnny Boy and then about ten years old, came down with pneumonia. This was long before penicillin. Dr. Hazen erected an oxygen tent over his son's bed, and sat by his bedside and ministered to him for three weeks, sending his own patients to Dr. Collins, Dr. Ransom and Dr. Mann, the other physicians in Brockport. John Jr. survived, went to West Point, graduated and lost his life the first night he was on the firing line in Italy in World War II. I was told later that Dr. Hazen never recovered from this loss and died not long afterward, a broken man.

It does not fit here chronologically, but does fit here with its geographic relationship to Dr. Hazen's office. Across Main Street from Dr. Hazen's home and office lived my friend Francis Comstock. I had a penchant for carpentry, but no talent for it. Francis had the bug too, but he had some talent. We spent hours at my house, scrounging lumber, sometimes lifting it piece by piece out of the house or barn or sandbox, and making something out of it. We tried to take out-of-sight pieces that no one would notice. The hayloft in the barn had been converted to storage for barrel parts for the Dad's produce business. We made lounge chairs out of barrel staves and Francis furnished most of the concept and execution. His Dad was the Postal Telegraph agent for our village. Telegraphy had an almost magic attraction for me, just thinking that a person could hit a key and send messages around the world. Brockport's World War II honor roll pictured in its 1964 Sesqui-Centennial celebration book lists Francis Comstock, U.S.N., as one who returned from the war.

Sister Emma became the first sadness connected with my stay with the Sisters in Brockport. I was puzzled when she did not return one week during my fourth year. A new Sister came. Sometime later that year, we learned that Sister Emma had died. I was devastated and heartbroken. There may have been advance knowledge of an illness among her co-religious or among elders, but no one warned a little boy who liked her very much. Except for the announcement of her death, I was given no information whatsoever. It was just a complete blank. She was gone and that was that.

There had been some good times, really good times. One-on-one instruction. Someone who cared, and who showed it. Rest periods from Altar Boy Latin instruction when I would be invited into the Sister's house for cookies. (It is a stretch to call that house a Convent, though it did have a small altar in the living room.) Between Sister Emma's loving instruction and my mother's unfailing ability to recall that "paper" she signed in the Rectory just seven years before, I became one of the Altar Boys that would be called upon for Solemn High Masses and ceremonies involving visits from the Bishop.

Sister Emma served the School of the Nativity of the BVM from 1906 to 1930. She died in the service of that school. My fourth grade year was 1929-1930. I was in retrospect lucky to have her for Altar Boy instruction and then as a teacher in the third grade. I have looked up the tenures of all the Sisters in that school and only Sister Martina (O'Reilly) who served from 1883-93 and again from 1901-29 served longer. (Sister Martina must have put in her final years in the convent. I do not recall her at school.) Sister Lucida, with an assignment from 1922 to 1931 was among the relatively few that had tenures over five years. Sisters were transferred without much notice due to shifting school populations. Sister Mary Joseph, my Dad's teacher, served as the Principal from 1900-09 and returned to BVM for another stint in 1918-24. It was about 1926 when my Dad introduced me to her. She was living in the Convent and occasionally helped out at school.

Today's pedagogy does not favor how I learned in Sister Emma's class. That class learned the times tables by standing at a blackboard competing with others at the board. Sister would rattle off the (m times n) problem and we would put the chalk to the board. Other times she would give the answer and ask us to put down all the ways it could be arrived at. By then we had developed the capability to visualize a virtual picture of the complete number set through thirteen, with a pretty fair knowledge of number sets up to twenty. Division followed quickly. Then it was on to multiplication of larger numbers and long division. Sister asked us to do our best and never criticized failure. She let us learn from one another. Whether the subject Geography or Spelling or Bible History, Sister Emma made it interesting to be in her class.

It was during my third grade in that school that I began to look ahead a bit to see where matters might be going next. With two grades reciting, I could listen to this year's lessons and next year's lessons. Sister Emma encouraged us first to think, and then to think fast. I believe now that my lifelong capacity for accuracy was a by-product of learning to "spit out the answers" or to write them down rapidly. There was no time to stand there and think of the wrong answer. I know that some of this method of learning is frowned on in some places but it worked for me then.

Years later, I felt right at home in competitive recitation as a midshipman at the United States Naval Academy. The slide rule we used there was a great time saving tool. But it was a confidence-builder to be able to make a fast check on its results by simply returning to the numbers sets learned in the third grade and asking oneself, "Is this answer in the ballpark?" Sister Emma's teaching methods left us with an enormous range of answers. The fact base we absorbed not only provided us a broad perspective on the positive side, but it was an effective antidote against fear and paralysis when the educational challenge provided something we had not previously encountered. Rapid reading became routine in order to stay in the game.

I do not recall learning anything about composition writing until later grades. We were "pupils" from the first grade but I believe now that I was on my way to becoming a student in Sister Emma's third grade at the School of the Nativity of the BVM. I came to school with no pronounced tendency to use the right hand or the left hand. The Sisters pushed the use of the right hand. The Palmer Method was taught from the beginning. A VP Cursive font (see illustration) is available from Educational Fontware based on a 1923 Palmer book. No laborious exercises now. You can do it with your computer.

Illustration 9 - Palmer Method Writing

I cannot fully account for the fourth grade. I have looked up teacher rosters by years and these suggest that I had Sister Emma for just part of the fourth grade and that we then had a new teacher for the last part of the year. It was Sister Emma for sure who prepared me for the "upper class" curriculum in Grades 5-6-7-8. She also helped get me ready for Sister Florentia, a commanding but holy lady who especially understood boys and helped them achieve their potential. Sister Florentia could roll with the punch but she knew when discipline and order were needed. She knew that the boy world would have some glitches along the way. She could always help get the ship back on an even keel.

Using a word I learned later on, our classroom days were marked by and large by décor. Order prevailed. Since we were lined up in columns by rows, the kids in the back could take in the whole perspective but they missed details that were evident to those up front. For example, someone was sent in from another class to tell Sister something. This was long before intercoms. That messenger would have to enter from the hallway by a door that was always toward the front of the room. Then there would be whisperings and well-tuned ears would be working overtime to catch words or phrases. Lip reading became a skill before any of us ever heard that term.

There were many examples of communication without talking. When the peace and tranquility seemed just too much, a pupil could "sign out" to go to the bathroom. This was done in a hand drawn square on the blackboard closest to the door. Imagine knowing by heart the initials of every pupil in your class. You knew. During such a trip, if you came from the back of the room you could see what was on Sister's desk. A boy in the back who saw that Jerry in the front had on the same sweater as yesterday could, by signing out to the bathroom, see if Jerry's sweater still had the chocolate spot on it. Similarly, a girl in the front could take the opportunity to find out if her friend Mary in the back was wearing the blouse with the lace on the sleeves. And of course, as a last resort, you could take your textbook to Sister and ask her what "that word" was. In half the cases, Sister knew you knew the word and that you needed, not only to stretch your legs, but to enjoy the fact that half the heads looked up to see what was going on.

As I noted, our family settled into the depression before October 1929. School was a welcome relief. For several years, home life was on a down slope. Food was always on your mind. Dad would go see a friend at the A&P Canning Company and come home with "bent'n rusties", cans that would never be sent out of the factory but could be sold locally for two cents a can. The canned goods menu included corn, peas, beets and even tiny potatoes. There were far too many lima beans. To this day, I cannot eat canned lima beans. Even when we all slid into the depression, the country kids from the farms always had food. Good food with a rich aroma, according to my nose. Occasionally I would get back to school after going home for lunch and some farm kids who had chosen to play outside during the first part of noon hour would still be eating. In addition to what I now recognize as a balanced diet with meat and a vegetable, all had at least two slices of bread with butter and jam or peanut butter. If the spread did not reach the crust, most ate up to the crust and then threw the rest away. That raised my eyebrows. Even after everyone was poor, back on South Avenue, the ladies would still make "finger" sandwiches, cutting the crusts off first. I always managed to be around. Whether it was Mrs. Raleigh with a catering job, or my mother or Mrs. Herbert Lane having a tea party, the object was to be positioned to eat those crust pieces. Mrs. Lane's was a favorite place. Shirley Lane was an early classmate. Mrs. Lane let me drink coffee and dunk her homemade doughnuts in it. Fabulous! In my own family, you guessed it, Dad ate the crust piece.

I suffered a little depression myself when it became clear that Sister Emma was no longer the teacher in the fourth grade. She just stopped coming to class and we had another Sister for our teacher.

Chapter Seven - Patriotism and Sister Florentia

Requiescant in pace.
Amen.

May they rest in peace.
Amen.

The title word "Patriotism" in this chapter heading does not do full justice to the extra-academic encouragement we received at Nativity of the Blessed Virgin Mary. Perhaps, "citizenship preparation" would better express some of the non-classroom endeavors we were encouraged to join. The Sisters wanted us to be good citizens.

Veteran's groups were prominent in Brockport. The recent war of 1914-1918 left young persons puzzled when their elders occasionally talked about their service experiences and especially about those who did not come back. In Mr. Dobson's Rexall drugstore up over the big mirror behind the soda bar, I would often gaze at a black and white photograph of a younger Dobson who had lost his life in a U.S. submarine tragedy. The VFW post in the village was called the Rodney Dobson Post.

Mrs. Harsch was a regular babysitter for Sis and me. She was a great storyteller in the evenings before bedtime. Her trip on the train to Chicago was my favorite. Sometimes Rosalie Harsch, Mrs. Harsch's daughter, who was studying to be a teacher at Columbia University, would take her mother's place. Rosalie would tell us a little about her father. There was a Harsch Crisp Seaman Post No. 179 of the American Legion in the village and I finally figured out that Mr. Harsch, and the other two men, had gone to World War I and had not returned. Rosalie furnished some fragments like this on her father that her mother never discussed.

Mrs. Harsch could make apple fritters. She also had currant bushes and brought us currant jelly that she made. Sometimes we would stay at her house. She had a sewing machine with drawers that contained all sorts of curious gadgets that fascinated me.

In the publication, "The Town of Sweden Sesqui-Centennial Celebration 1814-1964," there is reproduced a placard sponsored by American Legion Post No. 179 that lists, among other names of servicemen who served in World War II, the names James Dunn, John L. Hazen and Ralph L. Wallace. They were among my contemporaries in Brockport who did not return from service. I knew all three. Jimmy Dunn attended BVM a year or two before me. He lived on Centennial Drive, one of my later walking routes to the new High School. Leas Wallace lived just south on Main Street from the South Avenue intersection, across from the Lancashires. John Hazen, son of my Doctor John Hazen, lived just north on Main Street from South Avenue. He went to the U.S. Military Academy, graduated, departed for Italy and was killed in a mortar attack just hours after he had arrived at the front. There will be no Dunn-Hazen-

Wallace post of any national veteran's organization to remember their names so I decided to do that here.

Patriotic holidays were special events at BVM. These were celebrated at school the day before the day we had off. The only other day we had off during the school year was the feast day of St. Michael the Archangel. That Michael was the patron of our pastor, Father Michael J. Krieg. The sisters assigned special projects for Armistice Day, November 11, celebrating the end of World War I, for both Lincoln and Washington's birthdays in February, and for Decoration Day celebrated on May 30 each year. My favorite was Decoration Day because I could anticipate the town parade.

Some years there would be a day that was set aside for a school-wide patriotic event outside of the annual calendar of holidays. One such year we practiced a ceremony for receiving a new American Flag. Mr. Mulhern, a veteran and the Postmaster in Brockport, whose son Marvin was in my graduating class, arrived with a contingent of Legionnaires. From the Grade 1-4 student body I was chosen as the pupil to give the acceptance speech and from the Grade 5-8 classes, Betty Jane Elliott was chosen as the representative to speak. Sister Florentia, by then the School Principal, and Mr. Mulhern gave short talks. Betty Jane was next and I could see at once that the whole speech had departed from Betty's mind. Nothing came from her lips. Sister Florentia did not wait a second and moved her glance to me. We had rehearsed about a dozen times. The Sisters always wanted to be thoroughly prepared. I had the capacity at that age to listen to words and repeat them back verbatim. I gave Betty's speech and then my own and no one in attendance could have detected any glitch in the proceeding. Now, given that instant recall is no longer my forte, I keep the Missal open at Mass when I am the Lector or Cantor. That sense of obligation, inculcated by the Sisters, to stay alert to the current event has never left me.

That flag event was held in the school library. This was a tiny room and most of the attendees for the event had to stand out in the hall. There were not many books in our library. I read them all. There were few "classics" that I remember. All the Victor Appleton books were there. These included the Don Sturdy series and the Tom Swift series. In the former, "Don Sturdy in the Tombs of Gold" stands out. It gave me nightmares but I loved it. "Tom Swift and His Talking Picture Machine" was my favorite in that group. There were comparable book series for girls. I read them, too, but I did not broadcast the fact. Close to being regarded as a classic was "Wild Animals I Have Known." Author Ernest Thompson Seton. turns up in a current web search. I did find out later that "Victor Appleton" was a pen name.

There are organizations whose vigilance extends to keeping our state separate from any church. Stars and crosses are forbidden in holiday displays on state owned property. In our times today, a man named Barry Lynn will be on a TV station on a moment's notice if the station senses a church and state issue. His appearance decrying prayer in schools will be shown so fast that I sometimes feel that each TV station has a video tape of him ready to go. The Sisters love of their country was one of my most vivid memories of Parochial School. We pledged Allegiance to the Flag. We sang the Star Spangled Banner. We recited the great Whitman poem, "Oh Captain My Captain," while tears rolled down everyone's eyes. If all the subjects the Sisters taught had to be rolled up into one, it would have been called "God and Country."

I was perhaps eight years old when my family would let me attend the premier event of the year in Brockport, the Decoration Day parade. I was absolutely on my own and took full advantage of the complete freedom I was given on that day. I was a boy transfixed.

The parade came up High Street to the town cemetery next to the Brockport Cold Storage building. The cemetery was beautiful, freshly mowed, with plenty of trees for shade. I took a position on an embankment outside the wrought iron fence just short of the gate where the parade turned into the cemetery. There was a drum and bugle corps to help keep the marchers in step. Then came open touring cars, seven or eight passenger cars with no top.

Illustration 10 - Open Touring Car

Pictured in the Illustration above is an open touring car with its top up. For parades in good weather the tops folded down behind the back seat. Very old men with beards would be riding in cars like these. They were wearing fore and aft hats with white strings hanging down. These men were in the GAR, for Grand Army of the Republic, the Civil War veterans. Right behind them came marching men, some of whom limped a little and had a hard time keeping step. Their uniforms were a little rumpled looking and they carried no arms. They were Spanish American War veterans. Then came a marching band with full complement of instruments and players in good looking uniforms and metal hats. Immediately following this group marched squads of men, whose ranks abreast were dressed off smartly. These men kept up a brisk marching step. Like their band, they were fully uniformed with metal hats, and rifles on their shoulders with fixed bayonets. These men had just come back from World War I.

The parade turned into the cemetery, the marchers stopped and stood at parade rest, and a squad of riflemen fired three volleys. This was followed by taps played on a bugle, a real bugle, not a trumpet.

Day is done, gone the sun,
From the fields, from the hills,
From the sky.
Rest in peace, soldier brave,
God is nigh.

Those words are listed in most references as "Anon." Anonymous or not, I have the Sisters to thank for teaching them to me. Too many of the men they honor remain anonymous. Years later it was my duty to lead a squad of sailors into a cemetery in Oran, Algeria to lay to rest one Seaman Foley who had been a fire controlman striker in my Gunnery Department aboard the destroyer U.S.S. Edison. Navymen do not bear sidearms very often. We were completely respectful and somber and I had borrowed a military manual to help me give the right commands. But we were not precision sharp militia that gray day in 1943. Our rifle volleys did not sound as a single shot but had a little ripple movement effect and our bugler was trying to regain a skill he had set aside to join the Navy. Otherwise, though, I was reminded of Decoration Day at Brockport New York's town cemetery about 1928.

It took a few years after 1928 for me to develop enough perspective to enable me to identify the men in the parade groups. All I knew then is that they were soldiers. The American Flag that flew over the cemetery was full of holes. I assumed then that it was a battle flag that had been scarred by shellfire. Or that maybe the volleys from the riflemen passed through the flag.

Decoration Day, now Memorial Day, was school day off and Sister had made sure that each pupil knew exactly the route and time of the parade. We could anticipate that Sister would ask for detailed oral reports.

It was a disappointment to visit that cemetery during a 1997 trip to Brockport. The grace contributed by shade trees has gone. From its crowded appearance, the trees may have given way to a fully occupied plot of land.

The Cub Scouts and then the Boy Scouts had strong patriotic attractions for me. "Trustworthy, Loyal, Helpful" introduced virtues with overtones of patriotism. In fact, Parochial School, the Ten Commandments, and the Scouts all meshed together to form a positive path for a young boy's life. The fact that these came from diverse origins was never a question for me in those days. I know I needed every virtue-enhancing discipline available to offset some surely base instincts I knew I had. The Boy Scouts tested me in ways that Parochial School did not.

I entered the Cub Scouts at the first possible age, which I believe was eight or nine. I was being groomed for Scouts through a family friendship with Mr. Hiler, one of three brothers in the village who took an interest in young boys. Somehow, I actually joined the Cub Scout Den of Mr. .Reichel, a History teacher at the High School. That den convened once per week in the gym of St. Luke's Episcopal Church. Both Mr. Hiler and Mr. Reichel were outstanding leaders. I think I joined Mr. Reichel's Cub Scouts simply because he invited me to join. I soon discovered that Mr. Hiler was upset because I had not joined the Cub Scout group that was connected with his Boy Scout troop. None of the details here are important except the one of loyalty and doing what was expected of me. I never could figure out how I got into the bad graces of a man I liked simply because I did something he had not anticipated. There were plenty of times that I did not live up to expectations because of my perverse nature but this was not one of those cases.

Eventually I got into the Boy Scouts and made it to Star Scout, short of the Life and Eagle Scout level. To achieve the First Class Scout badge required a 14-mile hike. All roads west of Brockport led to Holley, New York. I departed with a group that headed west out Holley Street in Brockport. I never personally verified the distance but was informed that Holley was about six miles from the Brockport village limits. We camped in an empty field near Holley in pup tents we carried with us. We slept on the ground, our tents having no base flap. That meant ragweed, and rubbing my nose in my worst enemy. By morning I was into a full stage asthma attack and still had to walk home. The last segment was up the hill on Brockport's Main Street past the Hazens, underneath the railroad-bridge across from Coapman's gas station to the Rowe Coal yard. Main Street in

Brockport going south was a series of uphill grades. I was completely exhausted and had to stop in front of Jubenvilles just short of the Capen Hose Company at Park Avenue and Main. My Dad came by in a car. I was never so glad to see him and I gratefully accepted a ride the rest of the way. I'm sure I was a few tenths of a mile short of 14 miles. After a night of wheezing, those asthma attacks would level off. Morning brought me to Monday, and back to school.

Having mentioned my Dad and the Capen Hose Company in one sentence brings up my Dad's own association with Brockport's volunteer fire fighters. Although the Capen Hose Company was in our end of town and enjoyed the distinction of always having the most modern pumper, mostly Seagraves, the volunteer fire-company that attracted the most Irishmen was the Harrison Hose Company at the main downtown fire station. Dad became a member of the Harrison Hose Company. I found this connection to be of great interest. The Harrison Hose truck had classic lines, a ladder on each side of a long-bed truck with a powerful looking engine up front and room for two men in the open cab. The downtown fire station had four or five bays. Its center entrance led upstairs to "city hall", I was told. My only visit there was to hear my Uncle Vin who had come back to town to make a political speech for Governor Roosevelt. There was another pump-company there along with a hook and ladder company. If memory has not completely deserted me, the pump-company downtown was called "The Protectives." Volunteer fire companies enjoyed almost as much "mind share" in small towns as veteran's organizations. Dad was proud of his association with Harrison Hose. Each fire you did not get to you were "fined" $2.00 by your volunteer company. Dad's drinking caused him to miss fires. He was careful to pay the fines. Perry Shafer and Bert Thompson signed his 1929 Certificate.

Illustration 11 - My Dad Was a Fireman

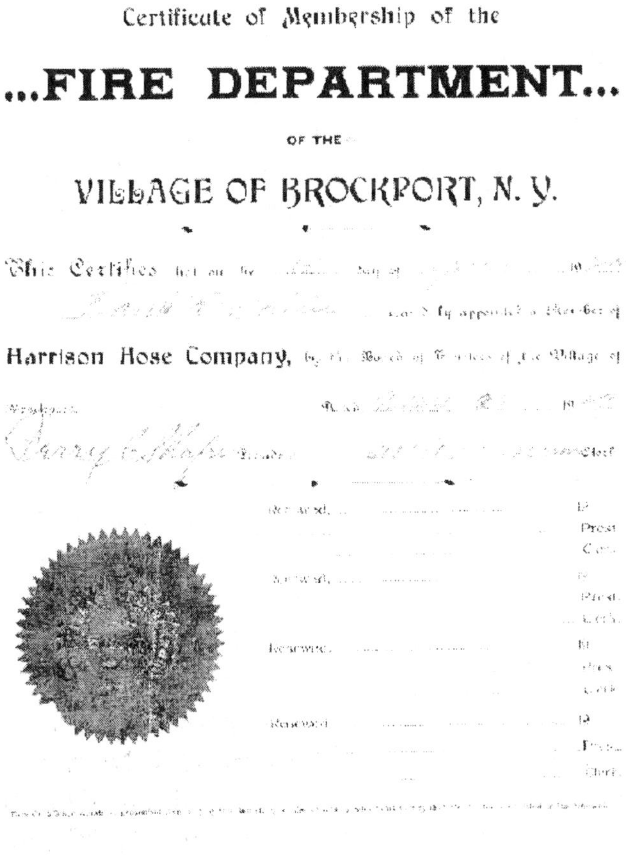

Certificate of Membership of the

...FIRE DEPARTMENT...

OF THE

VILLAGE OF BROCKPORT, N. Y.

This Certifies ...

Harrison Hose Company, ...

I should have added the YMCA to the list of organizations that are fixed in my mind as virtue building. The Scouts organized a weekly bus trip to the Arnett YMCA in Rochester and Sister promoted our participation, furnishing a list of Parochial School scouts interested in being part of the winter program. The object was to teach us all to swim. Captain Henry Jensen of the Rochester Police Force was our teacher. He was a big strong man and even if that had not distinguished him from 50 scrawny legged little boys, the fact that he wore swim trunks and we did not would make it clear who was in charge. And was he ever in charge. It took a little money even in those depression times to be included with the group. We went in a School Bus at night. The driver was a "volunteer." Captain Jensen knew of the financial sacrifices and made it his personal goal that we should swim. He not only taught us how to swim but how to administer the American Red Cross life saving technique practiced then. He taught the Buddy System and he enforced it. The foregoing activity was extracurricular to our Parochial School education but was aggressively promoted by Sister. Those were early life lessons I never forgot. These activities became part of my life as the result of my attendance at that Parochial School.

One Armistice Day event in 1931 was not on local calendars. In the dim haze and slight drizzle of a November 11th evening, from our back porch I saw the sight of my young life. It was the U.S. Navy dirigible Akron fishing her way back from Akron, Ohio to her Navy base at Lakehurst, New Jersey. By "fishing her way", I mean that she was up in what we later called "instrument flight conditions" for which she was not configured. Nor was the U.S. instrumented at that time. Her Navy pilot was using the south shore of Lake Ontario to try to get east of a weather band. Later, in a booklet, " A Resident's Recollections" by Lloyd Klos, about Rochester and Irondequoit, I read that the Akron spent an hour circling Rochester after passing Brockport. The weather then improved enough to make it directly to Lakehurst. Several other Nativity school classmates had seen the great airship. Sister suspended regular recitations the next day while every shred of information about dirigibles was shared. A couple of years later the Akron was lost in the Atlantic Ocean. Only three men survived. Not long after this event I saw Jack Holt, a movie star of those days, in a film called "Dirigible." The story was about a rescue attempt at the South Pole. An explorer group had made it to the pole. They encountered a blizzard trying to get back to base camp from the pole. Then, the one man they relied on for navigation became disabled and had to stay behind. Another man who believed he could rely on his own sense of direction in place of navigation took over. The climax came, when after harrowing days in the blizzard, the party arrived not at base camp, but back where their trek had begun. That movie gave me nightmares.

Two other aviation events remain etched in my mind. At the end of South Avenue down near Main Street lived the Peters family. A barnstorming aviator came to town. Steve Peters, then a young teenager and the Peters' only child, took the first ride with the pilot. The plane reminded one of the wood and canvas biplanes from World War I. The engine quit and the pilot crash-landed into the side of my dentist's brick home down on State Street. The pilot lived but young Steve perished.

The town of Leroy was the center of aviation in our area. It had one of the rotating light beacons by which planes could navigate across country at night in good weather. My Dad treated Mom, Sis and I to a flight about 1928 in a Stinson Detroiter, a high wing monoplane with a glass aperture in the cabin floor for looking straight down. Our pilot was Lieutenant Commander Russell Holderman, a WW I pilot who later became pilot for Gannett Newspapers' Lockheed Lodestar airplane. It was pay-before-fly. Dad took out a $100 bill for a 15-minute air tour of Leroy, famed for its Jello plant. He got $70 change. I figured later it was $10.00 for each adult and the kids flew for $5.00 apiece.

As it developed later, for the practical reason of money, I entered the Naval Academy in 1939. That was a year before the draft was extended by one vote in the House of Representatives. I served on active duty as a regular naval officer until 1956 and on reserve duty, as a naval aviator, until I was involuntarily "retired" as a Captain in the U.S. Naval Reserve. I then received a notice from the Draft Board in Palmer, Massachusetts, to report for induction. I had been in military service for 40 years. Viet Nam made the draft boards desperate for manpower. When I went to Palmer to see them (and they saw me), they found out why I had never previously been processed in the draft. They relented and let me continue in retirement.

Chapter Eight - Fifth Grade Turning Points

Et ne nos inducas in tentationem.
Sed libera nos a malo. Amen

And lead us not into tempation.
But deliver us from evil. Amen.

Our school was becoming very crowded. World War I baby boomers like myself filled every available seat. Fire drills came more frequently. The sisters were obviously concerned. No one used terms like "pupil/teacher ratio." The sisters took all students who applied. But the physical plant came under pressure. Exceeding sixty desks in a room meant narrowed aisles. I cannot recall any specific date in the fall of 1930 when I was in the fifth grade and Sister Florentia, the Principal, was now my teacher, that a search was announced to find candidates for skipping a grade. No one ever approached me directly but the effort to find candidates was not kept secret. I was already popping out answers in sixth grade oral recitations. I developed a reputation for being somewhat irrepressible. In the beginning, in frustration over a lack of answers she thought she had imparted to the sixth grade students, Sister did turn to the fifth grade side and see if there was a "volunteer." I loved to volunteer. Sometime during the year I was quietly re-assigned to a desk over with the

107

sixth grade. I have a vague recollection that this was preceded by a "parent/teacher" conference.

From then on, at the School of the Nativity of the BVM, my classmates were recycled each year.

That fifth/sixth grade year was not all roses. With Frederick "Buddy" Knight, who lived over on Fair Street that paralleled and was next to South Avenue, I had developed a trap line. Yes, those open jaw traps that are banned today. We prospected for muskrats (sometimes in our jargon, mushrats) and skunks. Despite the depression, there was a market for the pelts and Buddy's Dad knew where to sell them. Buddy had a .22 rifle in case we needed it to put an animal out of its misery. Sometimes we caught rabbits without intending to do so as their pelts had no value. Fortunately, Mrs. Knight could make great rabbit stew. Mostly, a rabbit would be gone when we got there early in the morning. They would chew their leg off at the joint above the trap jaw and leave it in the trap. One of our best places for a trap was under an old barn left abandoned when the new houses were built on South Avenue frontage in the late 19th century. One morning I discovered a pure black skunk in a trap we left in a foundation space leading under a barn floor.

Buddy was sick that morning and I was alone. No gun. Just me and a long piece of fallen tree that I wrestled loose from the undergrowth. It was about 5:30 a.m. on an early spring day. Frankie and his wooden club joined the fray against the skunk. That skunk fought like a tiger and dispensed clouds of perfume at every blow. I always knew the scent of a skunk but I had never seen it in fog form. I won, but the battle took an hour and it was getting close to school time. I retrieved my adversary and trudged home. Putting him in my hut in back of our barn, I got a quick breakfast and went to school.

We had just begun class when Sister Florentia called to me to come back into the Cloak Room . "Frank", she said, "I want you to go home and tell your mother to bury your clothes, give you a bath and get you back here as quickly as possible." "Why?" I asked Sister. "Frank, you are loaded with skunk fumes. The class will not be able to sit in the room with you and I know I can't."

So, as Sister directed, I went home, helped Mother bury my clothes, took a bath, dressed and returned to school. I guarantee to anyone, that if you have been on the battle line with a skunk, you will no longer be able to smell the stuff yourself. Buddy's Dad did sell the pelt. A perfectly black pelt, no white stripe at all, brought the trapper $1.00 in those depression days. That was a lot of money. It never dawned on me then that the buried clothes might have added up to more than one dollar. Money in the pocket was a countable item in the boy world. Buddy and I each had a 50-cent piece to show for our trap line efforts.

One feature of a pupil's life in the Nativity of the BVM School was the monthly visit of Father Krieg to every classroom to pass out the report cards for both classes. It was in Sister Florentia's fifth grade class that my memory of the event is most clearly etched. Father took Sister's place in her desk chair and she handed him the report cards, actually slim, brown cover booklets with pages for each month of the school year. Each page was divided into subjects. The inside front cover page contained your name and some other essentials. All entries were made in beautiful Palmer Method writing by Sister herself.

Sister Florentia worked just as hard with those who might excel as those who might not. Turn that statement around and it reveals the personal sacrifices she made. To many pupils who struggled, Sister contributed extra time at the Convent. Sister wanted the whole class to cross the finish line. In order to do this, she would work for weeks to get a slow learner from an F to a D. That was a triumph not only for the pupil but for Sister as well. And of course, it helped empty the classroom for the huge fourth grade coming up.

Father Krieg went by the book. His book. He never looked into the effort behind the result. The students with good marks received an "I expect this from every pupil." comment and the student with that D pulled up from an F would receive a lecture on how he or she was a disgrace to the student body. The student would take this rather hard. Rebukes, especially from the Pastor, had no redeeming value. Sister Florentia would just sigh and look to the heavens. I could tell that it tore her heart out.

Notwithstanding her dedication to accuracy, it was in Sister Florentia's classroom that I learned the only erroneous information conveyed by the Sisters in all my grade school days. In the sixth grade, we took a course called, "Civics." It was a half-year course and I found it very interesting. During a now forgotten President's administration back around the turn of the 19th to the 20th century, possibly that of Grover Cleveland, Sister taught us that the "spoils system" had been abolished. Sister, I'm sorry, but someone sold you a bill of goods.

The Biblical admonition, "Sons, do not cleave to your Mothers'" came up for adoption by me about this time. It was not planned this way. In the absence for lengthy periods of my father and her husband, I had been a partner with my mother in keeping a very large Victorian house functioning. For some time after he became insolvent, Dad was still the nominal owner of a coal business. Up to the point of total loss of the business, our basement would be filled each fall with about twenty tons of hard coal.

Blue Coal, a marketing name promoted by the coal arm of the Delaware, Lackawanna and Western (DL&W) Railway, was Pennsylvania hard coal with a blue dye sprayed onto it. It was a very long burning coal and was considered a good investment for heating if you could afford the cash investment to carry the inventory in your basement. It had fewer "emissions" than soft coal though it was considerably more expensive per ton. Dad's company carried Blue Coal, in several grades, as well as soft coal and coke. Another early advantage of Blue Coal is that it was advertised on radio by a creepy program featuring, "The Shadow."

It was my job to shovel coal into the mouth of our large, deep, double grate furnace. This long, rectangular furnace bed furnished the heat energy for a steam heat system. It took all the strength I could muster to get that coal back onto the second grate. It was necessary before reviving the fire in the furnace, to use a long portable lever to rock the front and back grates to dislodge the clinkers and then a long handled steel rake to even the bed of fire. We banked at night to save fuel, letting house temperature go down while we sought heat under blankets. There was an opening to the furnace in a basement side room to remove clinkers that could not be dislodged from actions at the front furnace door but it was necessary to let the fire go almost out to use this access. The final requirement of the furnace system was to check the sight gauge for level of water. Water was mandatory and it required manual intervention to open the valve. If the level was low, it was necessary to open a valve and raise the water to the required level, marked by a kind of rusty ring in the vertical glass sight gauge. Woe to me if I forgot to turn the water valve off! The radiators began spewing water that dealt the plaster in the ceilings an irreversible setback. All this background is intended to inform the reader that I was my Mother's partner for several years in keeping the house going during my Dad's periods of inebriation. I am proud of that partnership though Dad's binges made a somewhat fear -plagued person out of me.

One spring evening, friend Edwin Davis and I decided to visit his Dad who worked as a night mechanic at Judge's Ford on Lake Avenue in Rochester. We set off on our bikes for the ride. The weather was good, clear skies with no moon, and we knew the way. Our bikes had no lights but that was no impediment to night biking in those days. South Main Street in Brockport connected with the "Million Dollar"

Highway, Route 31, up at the "standpipe", a large vertical steel cylinder that held emergency water for the village. It was a marker of home for some and an eyesore to others. Here, Edwin and I turned east (left) and proceeded to Rochester via the town of Spencerport, coming into the city on Lyell Avenue. At Lyell Avenue's intersection with Lake Avenue, we turned south for a few blocks to Judge Ford agency. We visited with Edwin's Dad for a few minutes, and courtesy of Mr. Davis had one of those peanut butter and cracker snacks found in early vending machines, then left to go home. It was now about ten in the evening. Since we were not quite as fresh as when we left Brockport , the trip home took a little longer. It was about a 19-mile trip each way and we got back to the standpipe a little after midnight. There had been only about two cars pass us on the way back. Fortunately, the standpipe stood on one of the Lake Ontario escarpments on the south side of Brockport so, for the return to the village, elevation was in our favor. Our bikes rolled down that Main Street hill pretty fast. I turned off at South Avenue and Edwin went on to his home further into town. Thank God, no flats.

For the first time in my young memory, I was met at the door by a furious mother. It was only about one or two a.m. At first, I simply could not figure out what she was so upset about. She really let the prodigal son have it. I listened respectfully for about fifteen minutes and without confessing error and with a steely feeling inside, I went to bed unrepentant. In retrospect, I had helped Mom by replacing the head of the house in uncountable ways. I felt I had contributed. I did not have enough depth of understanding to realize that Mother could actually be worried about me. I was, I guess, moving on, and my mother's own characteristic lack of emotion was one of the traits I inherited from her. I am not proud of the fact that I have had to learn the virtue of understanding from my wife but am glad she has been there to help. I hope I have moved on in this respect. This has been an uphill challenge for me.

Chapter Nine - Seven, Eight and... You're Out

Ite, missa est.
Deo Gratias.

Go, the Mass is ended.
Thanks be to God.

As in Sister Florentia's room a year before, sometime during the school year 1931-32 I was moved from a seventh grade desk to an eighth grade desk. I did the recitations and took the exams for both classes. The room was even more crowded than our Grade 5-6 room had been. Families were moving into Brockport, pupils were transferring into our school, and some were being held back. There was another unannounced effort to get anyone who could move on to matriculate to high school.

Sister Florentia had taken Sister Josetta's place in 1930, replacing Sister Josetta both as Principal and as teacher of Grades Five and Six. Sometime during the 1931-32 school year, Sister St. Benedict who was teaching grades Seven and Eight left for reasons of fatigue. Sister Florentia took over the older classes and a replacement Sister came in for Grades Five and Six. The result was that Sister Florentia was my teacher for four grades at the Nativity of the BVM School. An examination of our graduation picture will show that I was the runt of the class among the boys. See, in the next Illustration, the short blond at the top left.

Illustration 12 - BVM Class of 1932

Each of us has probably had some moment of glory in life, but if the moment of glory above was passed without sufficient celebration, let me now celebrate each student above with the very minimum, their name in print. I will fail in one instance.

Top row, left to right, after the author, are dark haired Jerome "Jerry" Brinkman a great friend from the downtown section of Brockport, Art Ebert a great guy whose twin sister will be the last mentioned, Robert

Duff a friend to all, Longine Foltman whose name alone endeared him to me, Martin Mulhern with whom I played occasionally and Frederick "Buddy" Knight my Fair Street friend and trap line buddy.

Middle row, l-r, a very nice girl whose name I cannot now recall, then Mary Ellen Dailey, a favorite cousin and daughter of Uncle Oz, Ursula Luskey a very popular girl, Mary Bertha Pallace, another favorite cousin and daughter of my Dad's only sister Bertha who married Attorney John Pallace, Margaret O'Brien, Dorothy Booth, Lillian Moskowicz, and Leone Keable.

Front row, Betty Jane Elliott, Anna Pakula, Frances Petori, Virginia Hosmer, Father Michael J. Krieg, Betty Dailey, my cousin and sister of Mary Ellen, Dolores Duffy, Dorothy Brown and Lillian Ebert, Art's twin sister.

Mary Ellen Dailey and Betty Dailey had come to Brockport for just the final grades at BVM, having begun Parochial School at Blessed Sacrament in Rochester, New York. Mary Bertha Pallace was educated at home in Brockport and did not join us at BVM until the later grades.

Quite a number of these students came in on the bus from farming communities outside of Brockport. One result is that outside of their lunch pails with the tantalizing aromas, I did not get to know them well.

It is striking to me as I write these lines, with so much to say about the Sisters, that I note their complete absence from the photo. It is a disappointment. They received so little recognition. They gave so much and accomplished so much. They were missed, but only *after* they were gone. The professed Catholic teaching orders of the United States had been a national treasure. They had been taken for granted, not only by the Catholic Clergy, but by those who benefited the most, students and their parents.

A final comment on that graduation photo. Mother still had some power. For the photo event of this picture, she had the last word. I was wearing short pants. I was terribly embarrassed. My short stature and back row position saved the day for me, picture-wise. For every day that I knew her, my mother was an anglophile. She indulged this preference by visiting Toronto's department stores a couple of times each year to buy those wonderful woolens. Canada was her stand-in for "English."

The final year, 1931-32, events moved at a faster pace within the classroom irrespective of the crowding. Graduation was the objective and the effort became more intense. Pupils were introduced to the Board of Regents of the State of New York. Well, not personally of course, but by way of their first New York State Regent's examinations. For the certificate to move on to High School, a grammar school student needed a passing grade in two Regent's exams, Geography and Spelling. The successful completion of these examinations, with a mark of 65 or better out of a possible 100, was added to the requirement that you receive a favorable evaluation by your teacher based on your year of monthly grades for recitations and tests in all subjects.

The Regent's tests came in sealed packets to be opened by your teacher or exam proctor just before the time period allowed for the test began. There was usually a short instruction to be read aloud from the packet by the teacher followed by a solemn distribution of the examination itself to a hushed and worried bunch of boys and girls. This was drama of the first magnitude. It was a forerunner of the drama that would be played out each year in a New York State high school for much tougher subjects. Geography and Spelling were good icebreakers in that respect. Most of the eighth grade class where this took place were pretty well drilled by Sister in these subjects and few failed at this level. I am proud to say that I received a grade of 100 in Spelling and went to the New York State spelling bee held during the 1932 Rochester Exposition at Edgerton Park in Rochester New York. I am embarrassed to relate that I lasted a few rounds, then flubbed an easy word, "calculate."

One of my last student memories of Sister Florentia occurred as the result of an incident in the winter of 1930-31. Let me supply a little background. There were few companions for me on South Avenue. Howard Simmons lived directly across the street with his grandfather Elwood and grandmother Ida Simmons. They were strict Baptists and took a dim view of "goings-on" across the street at our house. But I was always welcome in their tiny home because of my friendship with Howard. The family read the Bible each morning and when I came they invited me to read, and I enjoyed that. In the summers, Howard was off to Bible

School each weekday morning. Now, Howard was not quite as dedicated to Christ as his grandparents but he did what they required without griping about it. The result was that he was not always available for playing. Up the street lived the Hanks family. Father Paul was an Attorney with two growing sons, Robert and Paul. Their ages were just under mine. A year older, as Howard was, or a year or two younger as the Hanks boys were, constituted major gaps for young boys growing up. My exact age matches were to be found in three boys over on Fair Street, and to be with them you had to be tough. Fighting, as in fist fighting or street wrestling, was a mark of passage. I was not tough. Still, if I wanted to play with them, the routine was that first the poorest fighter among them beat you up, then the next best and so on. The three boys were Fred "Buddy" Knight, Robert "Buster" Mosher and his twin brother Lewis Mosher. Since Fred Knight was my friend on the trap line, the unspoken agreement was that he would not have to beat me up. So, the routine for any day's play was Lewis would beat me up and then Robert would beat me up. They had a mean chow dog and sometimes they tried to get him to beat me up. After each day's ritual beatings were over, the four of us would play and have a great time. We played baseball, we hiked and made fires and cooked food over the coals. We spent hours in any abandoned buildings around and made up games to go with these presumably haunted structures. While I never became a good fighter, I got better as a matter of survival.

Illustration 13 -The Moshers with Buddy Knight

In Illustration 13, the boy at the top left is the same Buddy Knight shown in the BVM Class of 1932 graduation photo. In the center of the back row is Lewis Mosher and on the right is Robert Mosher. The two boys kneeling in front are Brad and Art Mosher. Those two were younger and I did not know them. Art Mosher introduced himself and gave me this picture when I gave and address at Brockport's A.D. Oliver Middle School rededication ceremony in 1997.

This winter day I was returning from lunch on my way to the Nativity of the BVM School. Another pair of twins, the Taylor twins, sons of a local minister, set upon me for no reason other than they thought they could beat me up. It turned out that I had become toughened a bit and their less adventurous life had not prepared them for someone who had decided on that occasion to fight to the death if necessary. After about 30 minutes, they high tailed it out of there, leaving me victor for the first time in my life, but also leaving me looking pretty bruised and a little bloody. I was late for afternoon class. I had to go see Sister Florentia in her role as Principal. This time, she took me to the boy's room to clean off some of the blood, then sat me down in the hall so the other students could not see or hear what was taking place. "Frank," she said, "I do not want you to get in a fight again and I do not want you to ever be late for school again." She waited for this to sink in and then she said, "Frank, if you absolutely cannot avoid those two the next time, give 'em one for me!" Little wonder that I had a love affair with Sister Florentia.

In an earlier chapter, I mentioned the Strand Theatre in Brockport, New York. Saturday afternoons there usually brought Tom Mix, Hoot Gibson or Ken Maynard, cowboy idols of many early "moving pictures." Occasionally, on Sunday our Dad would drive the family to Rochester for a movie and then dinner at Odenbach's Restaurant. Rochester had the RKO Palace, Loew's Rochester, the Piccadilly and the Regent, among its many fine movie houses.

I recall especially a short monologue from the final scene of one of those movies. George Arliss was the movie's star. He was a well-known British actor of the day. The film was "The Green Goddess." George played the Pooh-Bah of a small island nation tolerated by the Brits in their empire days to demonstrate that they did not control everything. The story put the lie to that. Seems that a British airplane with two pilots and one girl passenger had engine trouble and crash-landed on the beach of George's island. George, in his fancy turban headdress, was clearly in charge at the scene. He captured the three British citizens. A British warship with large guns showed up to demand their release. From the outset, it was clear that George had little interest in the pilots except to use them as bargaining chips to keep the girl, for whom he had developed a fancy. She was attractive, and chatty. The Brits sent a boat ashore and George expected the parley to begin. The British negotiator, a naval officer in gold braid with an overbearing, clipped, oral delivery, quickly made it clear that there would be no negotiation. All three would be released or the 16-inch guns of the warship would be ready to fire on George's little kingdom. The officer said he'd be back in a long boat for the captives in the morning. Sure enough, manned by many oarsmen, the next morning the long boat's bow came to rest gently on the gorgeous sand beach. George reluctantly released the pilots and the girl. As they rowed away, from his luxuriant palm grove on a cliff above the beach, George watched the proceeding with his long glass telescope. He then uttered the movie's closing remark, "She probably would have been a lot of trouble, anyway."

I departed from my beautiful little school in June of 1932. As I trudged back south on Utica Street for the last time and headed with my diploma toward home and in the fall to the Brockport High School, I do not recall any specific thoughts. In the years since, it has occurred to me that Sister Florentia, gazing out of her sixth grade window, might have had a thought for her 11-year old graduate similar to the closing remark George Arliss made from his island empire. The only difference was that Sister could have spoken with more certitude.

Chapter Ten - Epilogue

Requiescant in pace.
Amen.

May they rest in peace.
Amen.

My Dad became part of the Kelly family and the reader may recall a search I made with a Kelly daughter for a nursing home for my Dad with his incurable cancer. The Kelly family kind of fell apart in shock at the death thing. Probably the children could have handled it but Mrs. Kelly could not. Dad's last breath was announced when I was awakened by a phone call in the middle of the night by a caring Doctor in Rochester in late 1975 telling me that Dad had just gone peacefully in his sleep at the nursing home.

Mom got Dad back in death after a separation of about thirty years. She buried him and there were no Kellys visible in the mourning party. Dad went to Mass every day of his life during those last thirty years, choosing one of three downtown Rochester churches. His favorite was St. Mary's. He sometimes went to St. Joseph's until it burned down. In his final years he attended the French Church downtown. He was laid out decently and on a cold, snowy November day in 1975 a few mourners gathered at the French Church. I could tell that the Priest knew nothing of Dad's life but the Mass, as always, was beautiful. I was informed during the after Mass handshakes that no Priest could be spared to come to Holy Sepulchre. A Rochester motorcycle policeman escorted us all the way to the cemetery. Before leaving the church, I managed to filch a few missalettes when I realized there would be no Priest for the committal service. These contained some hymns. Some wonderful cousins, Vinny, Billy, Bobby, Donald A. Jr., Georgianne and Kitty joined Sis and Mom and me. At the gravesite, I handed out the missalettes, opened to a song page, and we sang together.

All the earth proclaim the Lord
Sing your praise to God.

Serve you the Lord,
Heart full of gladness,
Come into His Presence,
Singing for joy.

All the earth proclaim the Lord,
Sing your praise to God.

The Sisters were not physically present. But their always alert sense of presence, their inspiration for improvised leadership when required, certainly let my eye fall on those missalettes in the French Church and gave me the courage to appropriate them and use them for a worthy purpose. Besides, I was a little upset that no Priest could be found to make it to the burial site.

My father was definitely not a male chauvinist. I could cite his many more female friends than male friends. And I mean friends and nothing more. My birth coincided with the Suffrage Amendment giving women the right to vote in 1921. Dad took the time one day to advise me of his view of the suffrage change that many newspapers consistently referred to as the "emancipation" of women. Dad advised me that the right to obtain a driver's license was a much more liberating event for women than suffrage.

Born in 1897, my Dad was an acute witness to our nation's affairs as World War I was coming to an end. I have mentioned the Constitutional Amendments relating to the prohibition of beverage alcohol and the one giving women the right to vote. Dad did not handle the alcohol situation well and he had a lot of company. I had left his life when I entered the U.S. Naval Academy in 1939. I know now that he was then in the throes of his life struggle with booze. Prohibition had failed the nation. The Women's Christian Temperance Union, the WCTU, had had little success. The Alcoholics Anonymous movement came along in the late thirties and it proved to be the changing event in Dad's life. I cannot verify when he joined AA but the next illustration from his Gladstone bag establishes the time to be about 1941. Page -2- of this 1953 newsletter, not shown, mentions the upcoming 12th anniversary of the establishment of this Rochester chapter of AA. Also not shown is the Guest Editorial's byline at the end of the opening article. It was "Frank D."

Illustration 14 -AA Newsletter of 1953

EAST
DOES
IT

KEEP AN
OPEN MIND

FIRST
THINGS
FIRST

BUT FOR
THE GRACE
OF GOD

All Around ROCHESTER

A Monthly Bulletin of Events of
ALCOHOLICS ANONYMOUS issued from
820 Granite Building – Price 10¢

Vol. I – No. 1	ROCHESTER, NEW YORK	April 1, 1953

Guest Editorial

WHAT I BELIEVE

It does not matter much from what viewpoint an approach to A.A. is made so long as the candidate's heart is warm and willing. Nor does it matter from what stage in the alcoholic progress the problem child surrenders, so long as the decision is clear cut and without qualification. It is not a case of the end justifying the means. Once the seed of indoctrination has taken root, the growth to the end will be compelling. It will sweep aside all obstacles until at least some degree of peace of mind and tranquility has been reached. From there on progress will be less rapid, but there will be some progress till the end. By the "seed" I mean the first thought to make sense which the candidate can absorb in a cool, calm manner and with deep sincerity and realism. Even though it may be a case of the truth hurting the ego, the candidate at long last can feel a little relief in the discovery of how artificial he or she has been these many years.

The writer believes that when the first thought is made available to the candidate which appeals to his or to her honesty and sincerity, that at that instant the real test is on--shall we find ourselves out or not. Our decision at that time determines whether we shall embrace A.A. as a beautiful ideal or not. This in turn determines whether or not we reach some tranquility and peace of mind. Peace of mind only happens when A.A. thinking makes us rather than we making A.A. We have nothing to say about this stage of our progress because it is accomplished for us. The test which the writer refers to above is no time for the candidate to reach down into his bag of tricks. Phony aspirations and unusual emotions will defeat our purpose. When the test arrives, we must accept it with honesty or dishonesty. If we decide to accept the horrible truth about ourselves rather than continue the old nightmare, the end from that point on is never in doubt. A process of this kind of constructive thinking leads us to love and service, kindness towards other humans and happiness here to the extent of our capacity.

The writer feels that many alcoholics never reach the test in A.A. thinking. They may stay dry for many years through A.A. group therapy or sheer determination without facing the test. These people never seem to be happy in their sobriety. The writer believes that the candidates who eventually receive A.A. happiness are those who find themselves happier in their sobriety than they were formerly in their alcohol. It seems that this is necessary for a member to be so-called "fool-proof" from alcohol.

The year after Dad's death in 1975, I was fortunate to be able to re-visit the Sisters in their home territory. This came about courtesy of a letter from Noel Myers (Mrs. Raymond Myers), then of 27 Kimberlin Drive,

Brockport, N.Y. In the letter, penned in a strong writing style with Palmer Method structure still evident, Noel thanked me for the check for my reservations to the 1976 Centennial Dinner for the School of the Nativity of the Blessed Virgin Mary. She informed me that Sister Lucida would be attending but that Sister Florentia could not attend as she was by then a patient at the Infirmary at the Mother House in Pittsford, New York. Noel had called the Mother House to see if I could visit Sister Florentia there and in her letter to me of May 11, 1976, I was told that Sister "will be expecting you." Noel also told me that my request that the organist play "Bring Flowers of the Fairest" at the Mass for the 100th anniversary occasion had been passed along to the lady organist. My memory is that it was not played but "O Sanctissima" was played at the Offertory. "Bring Flowers..." had been a great favorite during my stay at the school and Noel Myers seconded that sentiment in her letter.

If pressed, I do not know whether "Bring flowers..." or "O Captain, My Captain..." would be my favorite from those days in Parochial School. The Sisters constantly brought beautiful words to our attention. We sang, we recited, we read.

Before arriving at this wonderful 1976 celebration in Brockport, I stopped in Pittsford N.Y. at the Motherhouse of the Sisters of St. Joseph. I had brought two of my boys along to keep me company and to give them an insight on a great era for Catholic education, an education which some of my older children had enjoyed depending on what part of the U.S. we lived in when they were of age. The two children that came with me on that trip were John, number five, and Vinnie, eighth and last. Both were well over six feet tall when we headed from western Massachusetts to Pittsford, New York, located on the eastern fringe of Rochester.

The 320-mile drive from Springfield was uneventful and we arrived at the Infirmary at the Motherhouse in good time. The Sisters were still wearing habits. A smiling, young Sister at the Reception Desk welcomed us. Yes, we could go right up to see Sister Florentia as the staff had known of our coming and all was in readiness. "Just one matter, Mr. Dailey, that you may not have been made aware of. Sister has not known anyone for a few years although she is in reasonably good physical health. Go right up to her room." I was a little uneasy, not having thought out a protocol for this kind of meeting. I had not seen this lady for over 40 years.

We walked into her room. Immaculate, as was she in a modified habit suitable for a bed patient to receive visitors. Her head was on a puffed-up pillow so that she was not fully reclining. She looked just like the Sister Florentia that I had come to love and to respect. I began a monologue about auto travel and weather (it was a beautiful day in spring) and her eyes opened slightly and fell upon my sons. I could see that there was no glimmer of recognition of these strange boys but blessedly no hint of alarm in her gaze. Finally, I moved the subject toward someone we both had known. "Sister", I said, "Do you remember Father Krieg?" I had used the "magic word" to borrow a term from an early television show.

She bolted up to a sitting position. "Frank," she said, "He was no good!" With that, the dialogue began at a furious pace. She had worked so hard to give every pupil a chance to learn and to increase their confidence that they could learn. Father had consistently failed to acclaim or even acknowledge any effort along this line. He directed that she stick to a policy of rigid number evaluations based on day by day school recitation and examination without regard to an individual's family background or living environment. Father wanted no unpleasant discussions with the civil authorities, one of whom actually countersigned every BVM school certificate of advancement before it took effect in the New York State education system. (I have my sister's eighth grade graduation certificate in 1935 and mine from 1932, both countersigned by the appointed state official of that period.) Sister told me of her repeated efforts to get her Superior in the Sisters of St. Joseph in Rochester to assign her to another parish school. Looking at the record, Sister Florentia served just three years in Brockport, two of them covering my last four grades in school. So, her entreaties to leave were finally successful in 1933, a year after I had left for high school.

Sister also told me the name of the family she had come from (Smead) and the town (Geneva, N.Y.) that she had grown up in. She had entered the Sisters of St. Joseph from the St. Frances de Sales parish in Geneva, N.Y. in 1909 and had a younger sister, Anna de Sales who was also a Sister of St. Joseph. Sister Florentia had served 60 years covering seven elementary schools in the Diocese of Rochester, the last being at Holy Rosary parish. For thirty minutes we talked together in an animated and at times tearful conversation. I realized finally, though I hated to leave, that I must not tire her out. I brought the dialogue to a close, the boys respectfully said good bye, and we left and went back down to the lobby. The young Sister was still at her Reception Desk. I had the momentary thought that I might tell her that Sister Florentia had full possession of her faculties, but again, the Guardian Angel must have overcalled me. I left knowing that the young Sister would be able to go on with her duties without any unsettling thoughts.

An obituary in the Rochester Democrat & Chronicle noted Sister Florentia's date of death on February 20, 1985 after 11 years in that Infirmary. The obituary notice stated, in part, "Sister Smead was one of those rare and dedicated teachers who had discipline when required, sympathy when needed; counsel when wanted and love at all times." Someone obviously knew Sister well. The right person wrote those lines. My sharp-eyed Mother, then 86 herself and living independently in a Rochester apartment, sent Sister Florentia's newspaper obituary notice along to me. Sister Florentia was 93 when she died. My Mom died in 1992 at the age of 93. She and Sister Florentia were of like minds in the discipline matter. Sister Florentia had a little the better of it with her Irish sense of humor.

Sister Lucida Rice passed on December 30, 1989 in the Sisters of St. Joseph Convent Infirmary in Pittsford, New York. She had been born in Ithaca, New York, and entered the order in Rochester in 1918. She taught at seven Rochester Diocese schools, including a term as Principal at St. John, The Evangelist, in Spencerport, New York. Her obituary declared her to be a lively person and an excellent teacher, concluding, "She always brought out the best in her students." Amen.

Isabel Lasher Dailey passed at the Eagle Pond Nursing Home in Dennisport, Massachusetts on May 9, 1992. Her daughter, Alma Dailey Valentin, passed at the Cape Cod Hospital in Hyannis, Massachusetts on December 11, 1999. After forty years of geographic separation, Sis and her Mom had one last year together in the same apartment house in Dennisport before Isabel's slow onset of dementia required around the clock care. Sis told me that a week before Mother's death, during her last visit with her, Mother had said, "Tell Frankie I love him." Isabel recited the Our Father with me on the phone the day before her death at the Nursing Home, finishing it with the triumphant, "For Thine is the Kingdom, the Power, and the Glory of God, forever and forever, Amen." That ending was much preferred by her to the Roman Catholic Lord's Prayer that ended several words sooner.

The Holy Sepulchre Roman Catholic Cemetery on Lake Avenue in Rochester borders the Genesee River. 11 bodies were re-interred in that cemetery when the Dailey plot opened in July of 1917. Among those brought from other sites were John and Mary Dailey who came from Ireland in 1836. They were my Dad's grandparents. John was born in 1805 and is the oldest resident of the Dailey lot. The original lot was laid out for 50 gravesites. With infants, and now the permission for cremation in the Catholic Church, the population is already much larger than 50. There are still several open sites. The central message is one of couples. There are spinster ladies and second wives, but couples are predominant. Where couples and their children lie, a story is told in the unusually detailed inscriptions.

My Dad is there, but Mother is not. She chose to be with her parents in Riverside Cemetery, adjacent to and downstream of Holy Sepulchre. Except for chance tellings in pages such as these, Dad's marriage story will always remain incomplete at Holy Sepulchre. A piece of the tapestry will return in a few days. My Sis will be buried next to her father.

God has given me the gift of wonderful ladies. One of these is my own wife, Marguerite "Peggy" Parker. We are now in the 57th year of marriage. As was her custom, my mother stood aloof to any lady until she was very, very sure of her ground with that lady. My wife, of southern origins, proved to be no exception. My mother never had a better friend than my wife and it probably took Mom only about 25 years to figure that out. My Sis was immediate in her recognition that she had found a lifetime friend in my wife. Sis accorded Peggy Sis' own special nom de plume, "Peggity."

Go back into your old Parochial School when all is quiet. Listen. Hear your Sister in the walls.